LISZT - Very Best
for piano

Franz Liszt
(1811-1886)

Catalog #07-2036

ISBN# 1-56922-094-8

Printed in the United States of America

Produced by John L. Haag

Exclusive Distributor for the Entire World:
CREATIVE CONCEPTS PUBLISHING CORP.
2290 Eastman Avenue #110, Ventura, California 93003

Franz (Ferencz) Liszt 1811-1886

Liszt was born in Raiding, Hungary, and grew up in a musical environment —his father was an official at the Esterházy court where Haydn had worked. The family soon moved to Vienna, where Liszt studied the piano with Carl Czerny and composition with Mozart's rival, Antonio Salieri. At a concert given in the presence of Beethoven, Liszt is said to have been rewarded with a kiss on the forehead from the aging master.

In 1823 Liszt arrived in Paris, where he soon became a celebrated performer and toured France. In 1824, he also played in England, where he was received by King George IV, before illness and the death of his father from typhoid prompted his return. In 1826, he went back to Paris, where he befriended Berlioz and Chopin and began his career as a progressive and visionary composer. He also considered becoming a priest and in addition to everything else fell in love —these three sides to his character competed for ascendancy during the rest of his life.

As a composer Liszt was influenced by leading Romantics, such as the author Victor Hugo and the painter Eugéne Delacroix; while Chopin brought out his poetic nature, Berlioz encouraged the latent Mephistophelian character in his music. On hearing Paganini's playing in 1831, Liszt set out to match the violinist's astonishing virtuosity in his own work, and wrote a piano transcription of Paganini's *La Campanella*. These diabolical and fiendishly virtuoso elements would later find expression in the swirling *Mephisto Waltzes* for piano.

In 1834, Liszt began a long affair with the Countess Marie d'Agoult, and the couple moved to Geneva the following year. He continued to perform widely, and won a famous piano duel against his rival Sigismond Thalberg in 1837. In 1839 he began touring extensively as he sought to raise funds for a Beethoven memorial in Bonn. His piano playing created a sensation wherever he went. He was honored in his native Hungary, where he rediscovered the interest in gypsy music that would later inspire his *Hungarian Rhapsodies*. He also proposed the establishment of a national conservatory in Budapest. But his long absences from home cost him his relationship with the countess, and they separated in 1844.

In 1847, the Princess Carolyne Sayn-Wittgenstein of Kiev persuaded him to give up traveling and settle as a full-time conductor and composer in Weimar, Germany. In the course of the next 12 years he conducted music by Wagner (including the first performance of *Lohengrin* in 1850), Schumann, Berlioz, Verdi, and others, in addition to performances of his own works. Weimar became the shrine of the 'New German School,' and pianists and composers flocked there for lessons or consultations with Liszt, for which he refused payment. However, his cohabitation with the married princess was becoming a court scandal, and his enthusiastic support of Wagner (then a political exile) was highly controversial. He resigned his post in 1858 and eventually left Weimar in 1861.

Liszt is credited with the invention of the symphonic poem, and he completed all but one of the works employing this quintessentially Romantic form during his Weimar years. The main technique was 'thematic transformation,' in which one or more musical themes, representing heroic people or ideas, evolved throughout the work, providing both musical structure and Romantic narrative. The technique reached its zenith in his *Piano Sonata in B Minor* (1853) and in the *Faust Symphony* (1854).

Liszt eventually joined Princess Carolyne in Rome. He remained there for eight years, occupying himself mainly with music inspired by religion, including the reflective *Années de pèlerinage* (Years of Pilgrimage) for piano. These pieces are in three volumes: the first deals with Swiss subjects, the second with Italian, and the third is an unauthorized volume published after Liszt's death. In 1865 he took the four minor orders of the Catholic Church.

Invitations to Weimar in 1869 and to Budapest in 1871 marked the beginning of a new phase in his life, and he subsequently traveled continually between these two cities and Rome. The three centers symbolized the visionary artist, the passionate gypsy, and the pious Catholic that lived within the same man.

Liszt's final tour in 1886 took him once again to Paris and London, but he soon became weak with dropsy and spent his last days in the Wagner festival town of Bayreuth. There he was looked after by Cosima, his second daughter by the Countess d'Agoult and by then Wagner's widow, and was able to attend a production of *Parsifal* before dying from pneumonia. Liszt left behind more than 400 original works in addition to many transcriptions and arrangements, and he made an impact during his life as the most phenomenal pianist of his time.

LISZT · Very Best for piano

Contents

BY THE LAKE OF WALLENSTADT (From the Suite "Years of Pilgrimage").........8

CONSOLATION NO. 1 12

CONSOLATION NO. 2 16

CONSOLATION NO. 3 20

CONSOLATION NO. 4 24

CONSOLATION NO. 5 13

DANCE OF THE GNOMES 26

(The) ERL KING (A Transcription of Schubert's Melody)............................36

ETUDE NO. 11 (Evening Harmonies)..42

ETUDE IN E (From the Suite "Years of Pilgrimage")..............................54

FAREWELL (Abscheid)..60

FUNERAL PROCESSION OF GONDOLAS NO. 1 62

FUNERAL PROCESSION OF GONDOLAS NO.2 66

HUNGARIAN RHAPSODY NO. 2 72

HUNGARIAN RHAPSODY NO. 6 86

LA REGATTA VENETIANA (Nocturne)..96

LIEBESTRAUM NO. 1 102

LIEBESTRAUM NO. 2 108

LIEBESTRAUM NO. 3 112

MEPHISTO WALTZ (Theme)..118

NOCTURNE IN B (En Reve)...120

NUAGES GRIS 122

VALSE MELANCOLIQUE 124

VALSE OUBLIEE NO. 1 130

WALDESRAUSCHEN (Konzert-Etude)..136

1845

1846

1856

1871

BY THE LAKE OF WALLENSTADT
(From the Suite "Years of Pilgrimage")

Franz Liszt
(1811-1886)

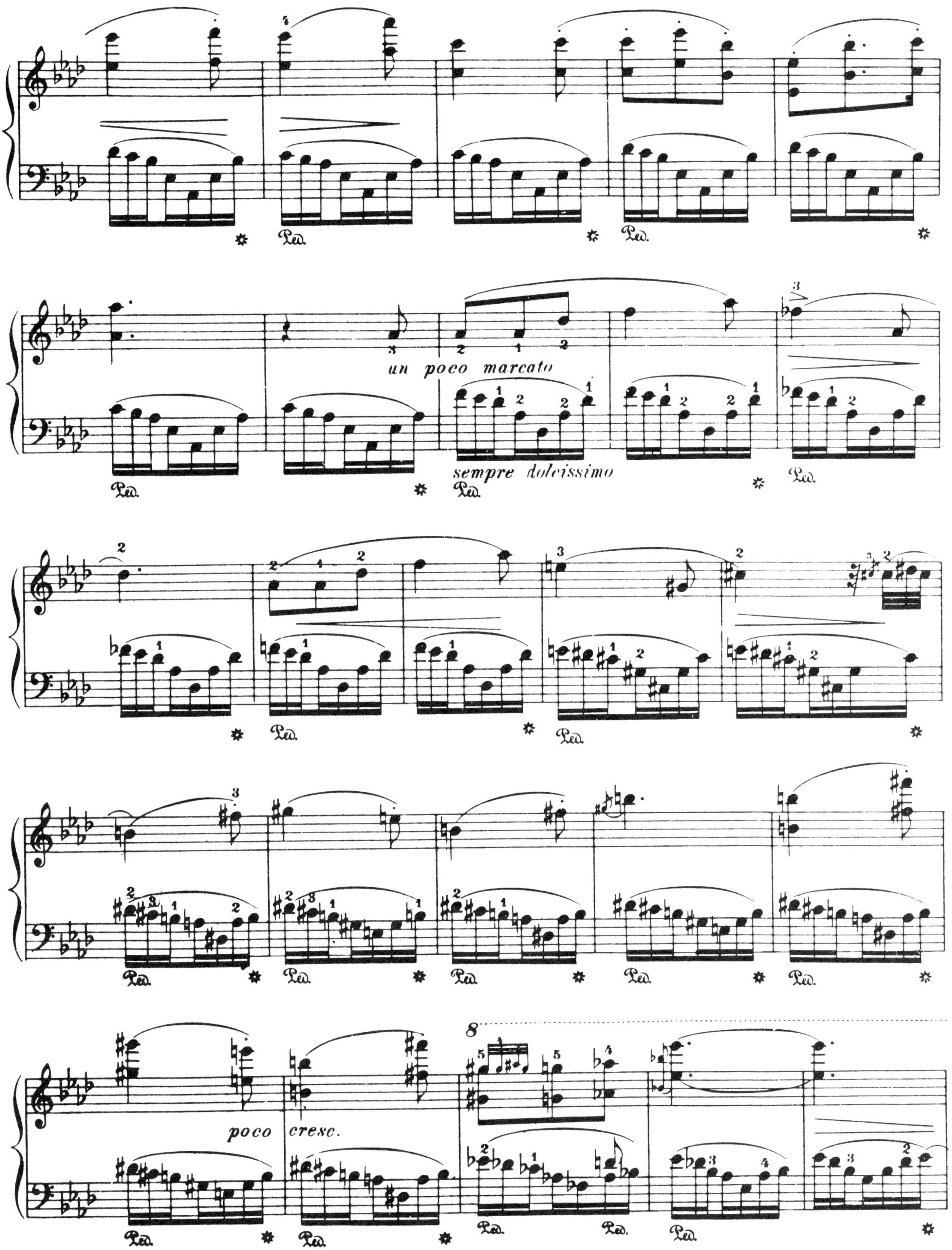
un poco marcato
sempre dolcissimo
poco cresc.
8

perdendosi
un poco più animato
più forte la mano destra
cresc.
poco rallentando
Ped.

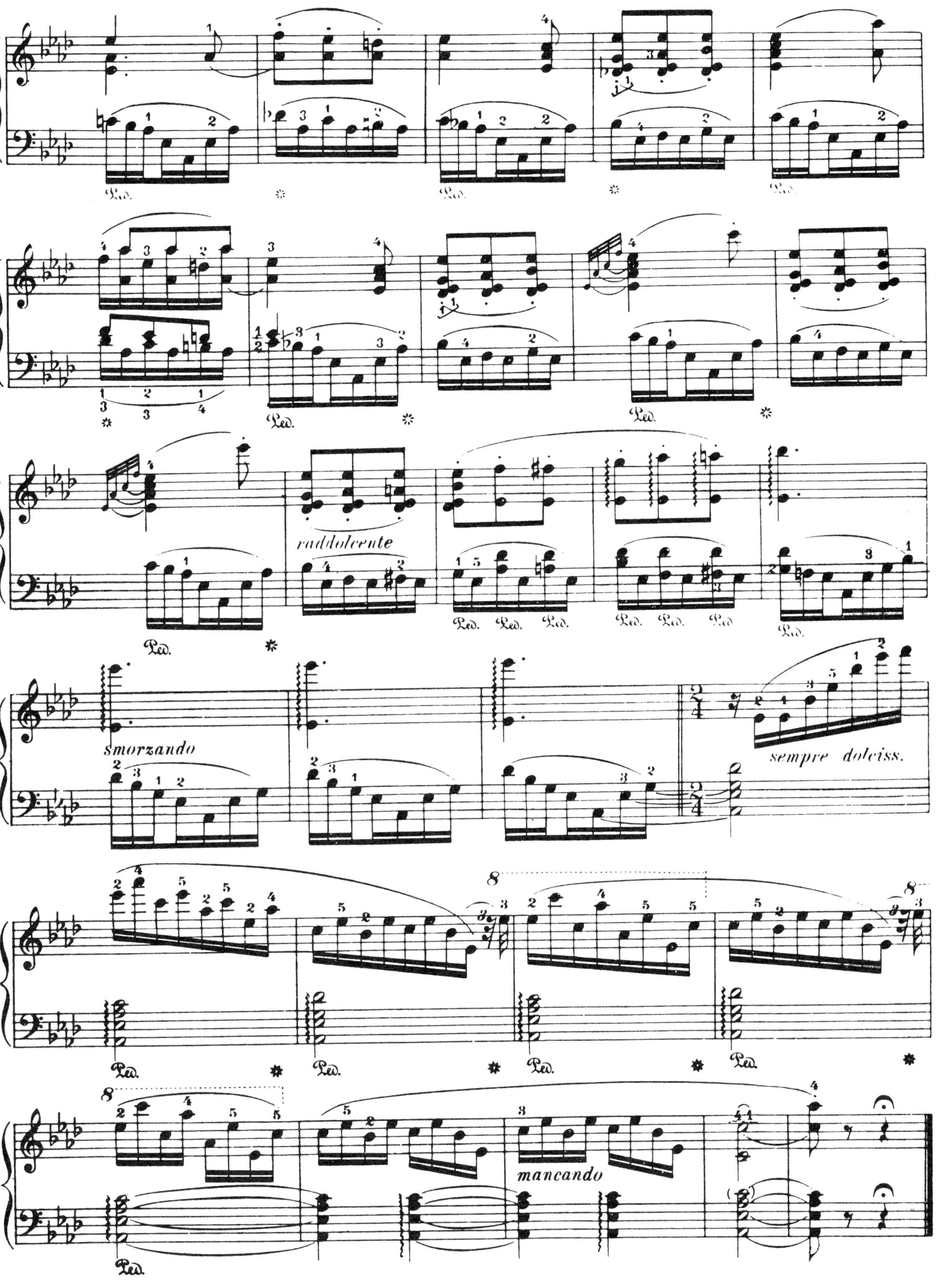
raddolcente
smorzando
sempre dolciss.
mancando

CONSOLATION NO. 1

Franz Liszt
(1811-1886)

CONSOLATION NO. 5

Franz Liszt
(1811-1886)

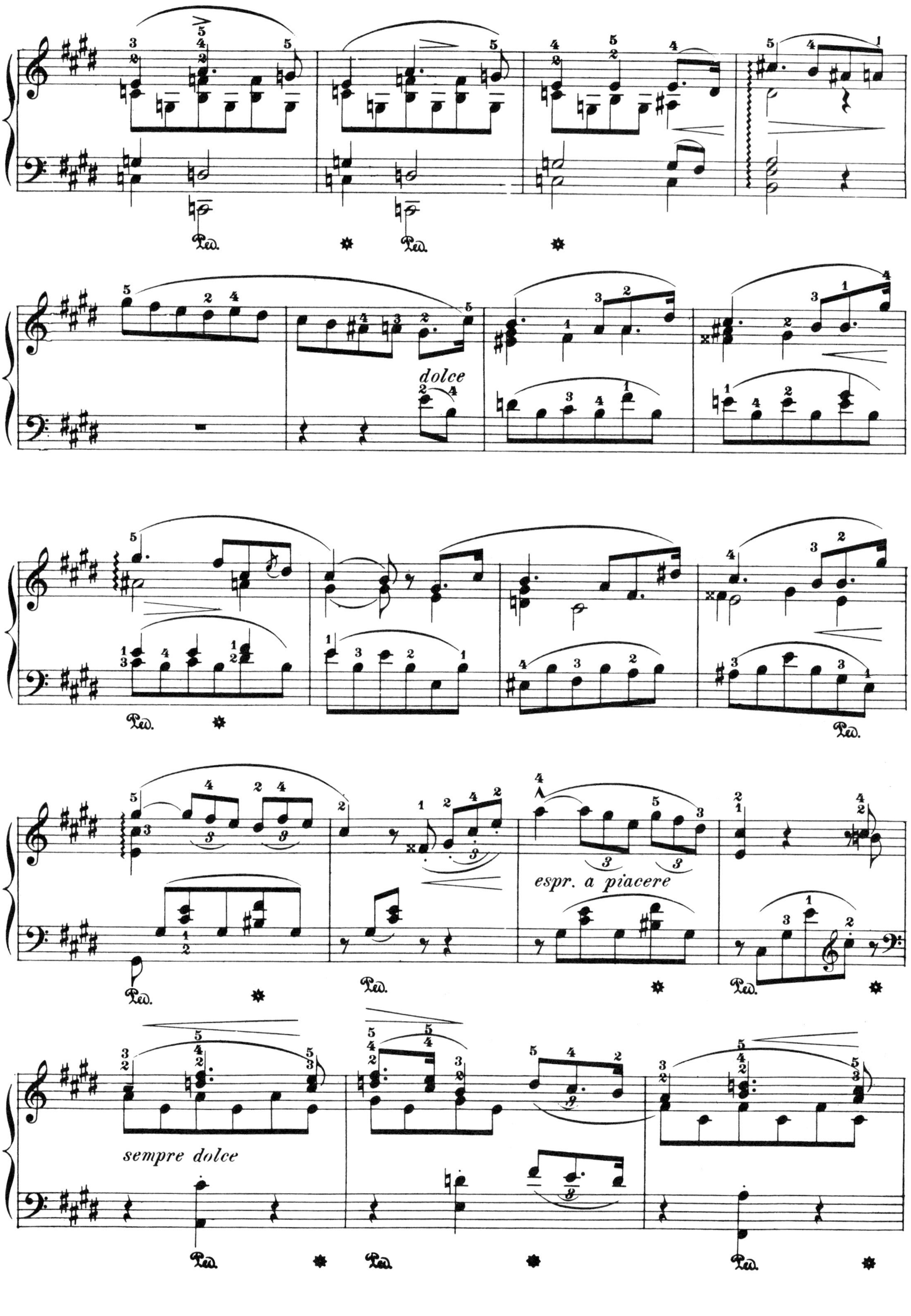
dolce
Ped.
espr. a piacere
sempre dolce

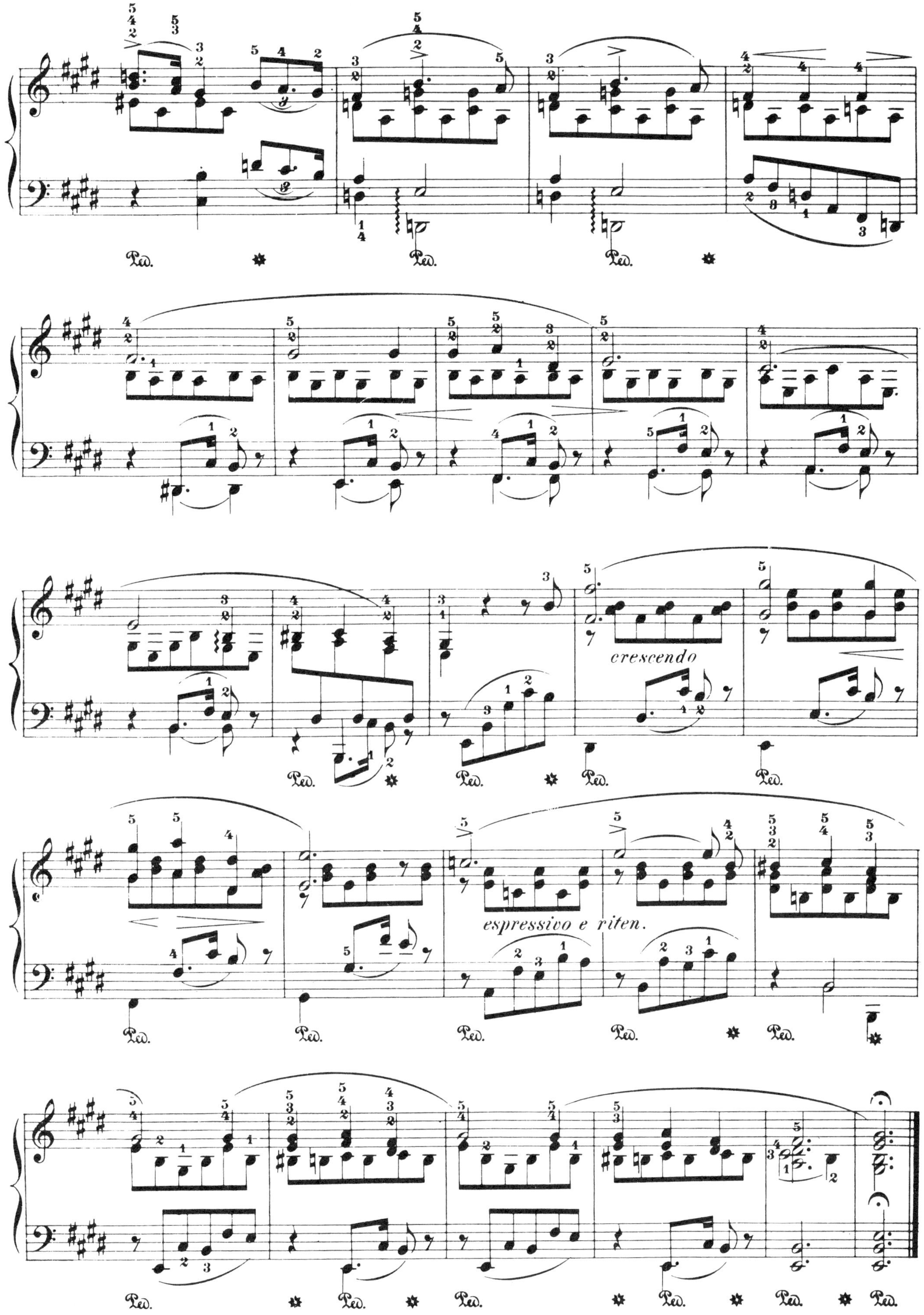
crescendo
espressivo e riten.

CONSOLATION NO. 2

Franz Liszt
(1811-1886)

Un poco più mosso

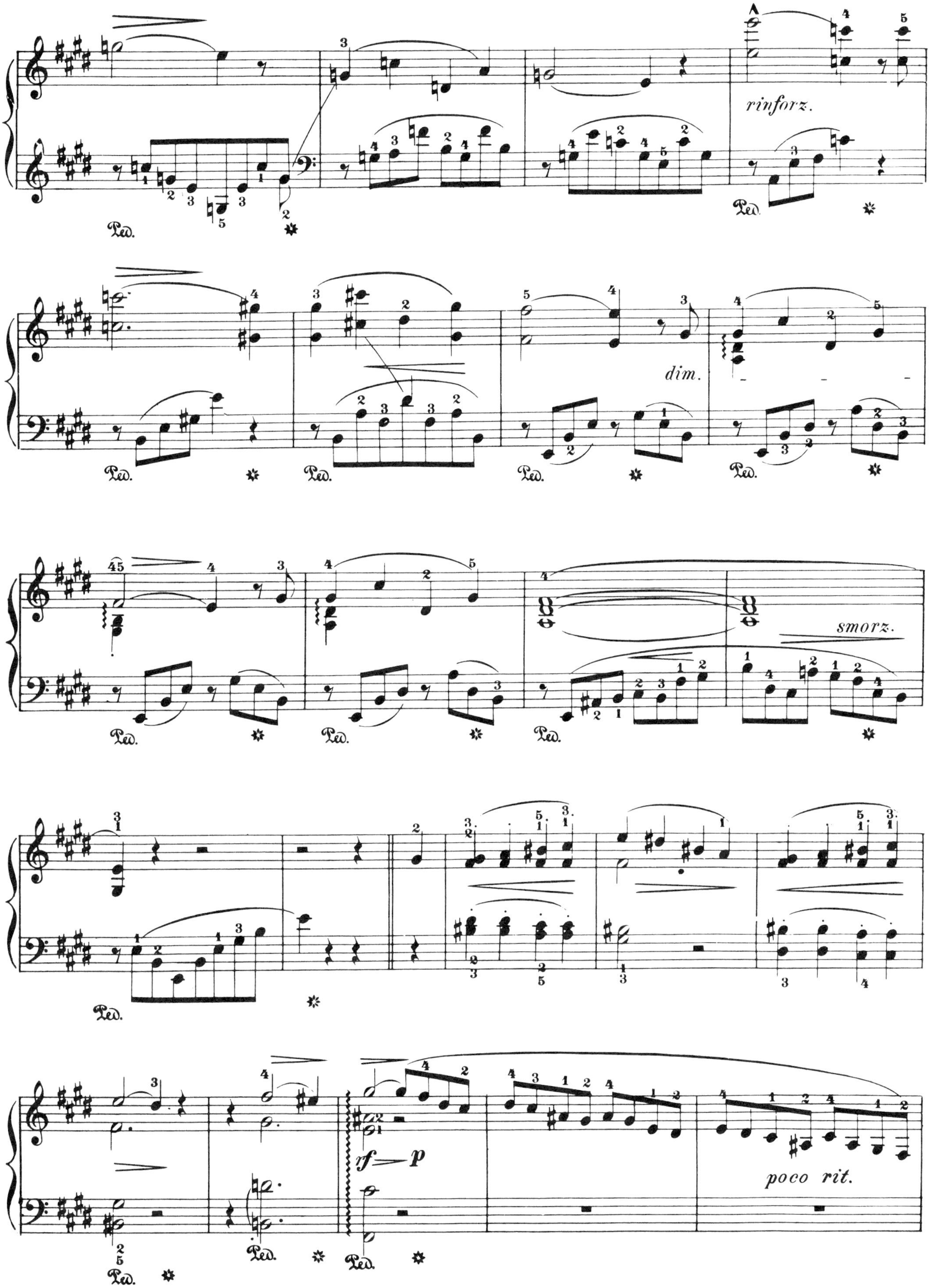
rinforz.
dim.
smorz.
rf p
poco rit.
Ped.

a tempo
ben marcato ed espressivo il canto
smorz.
cantando
appassionato
poco rit.
accentato ed espressivo assai
smorz.

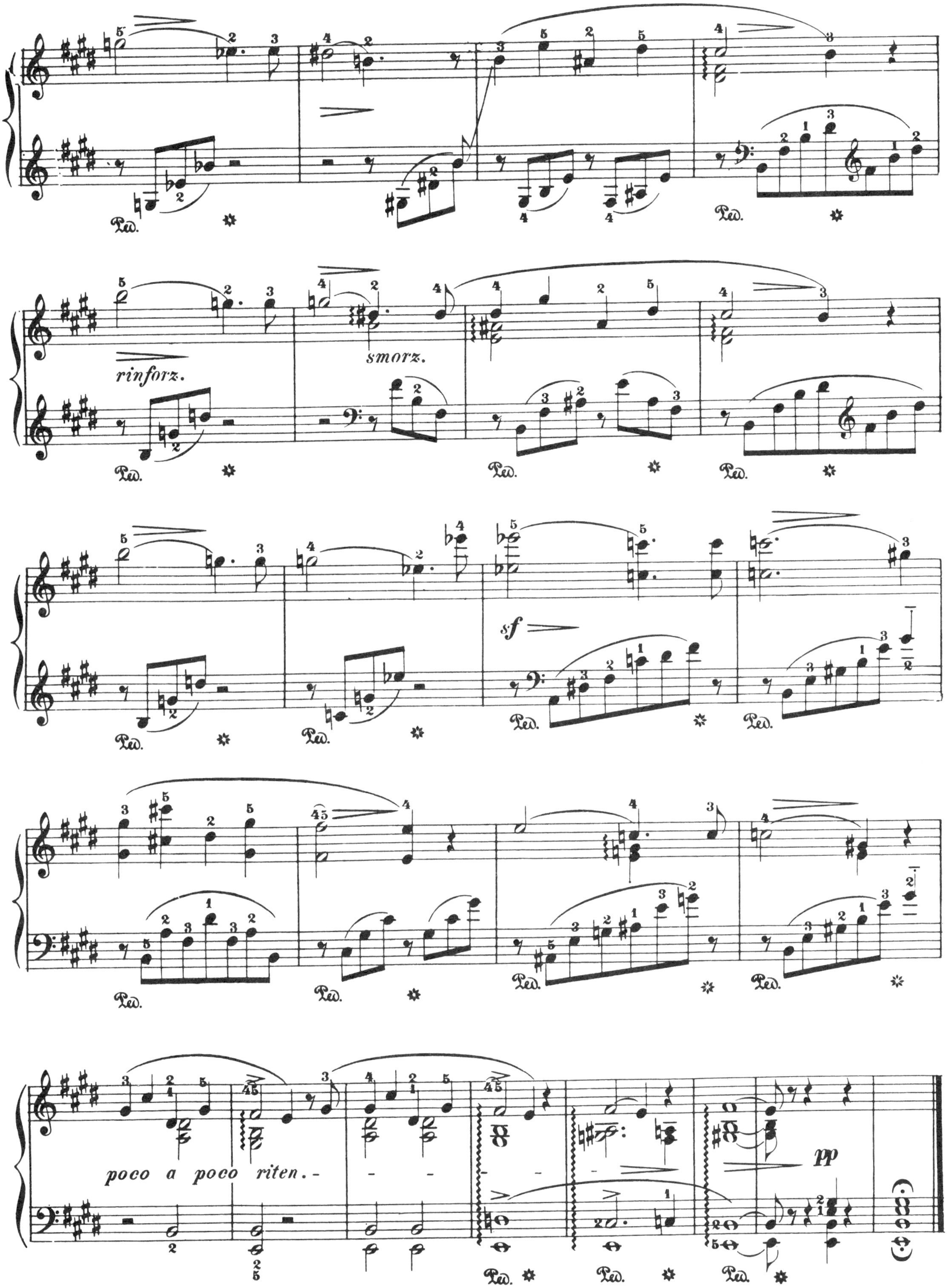
rinforz.
smorz.
sf
poco a poco riten.
pp
Ped.

CONSOLATION NO. 3

Franz Liszt
(1811-1886)

Lento placido

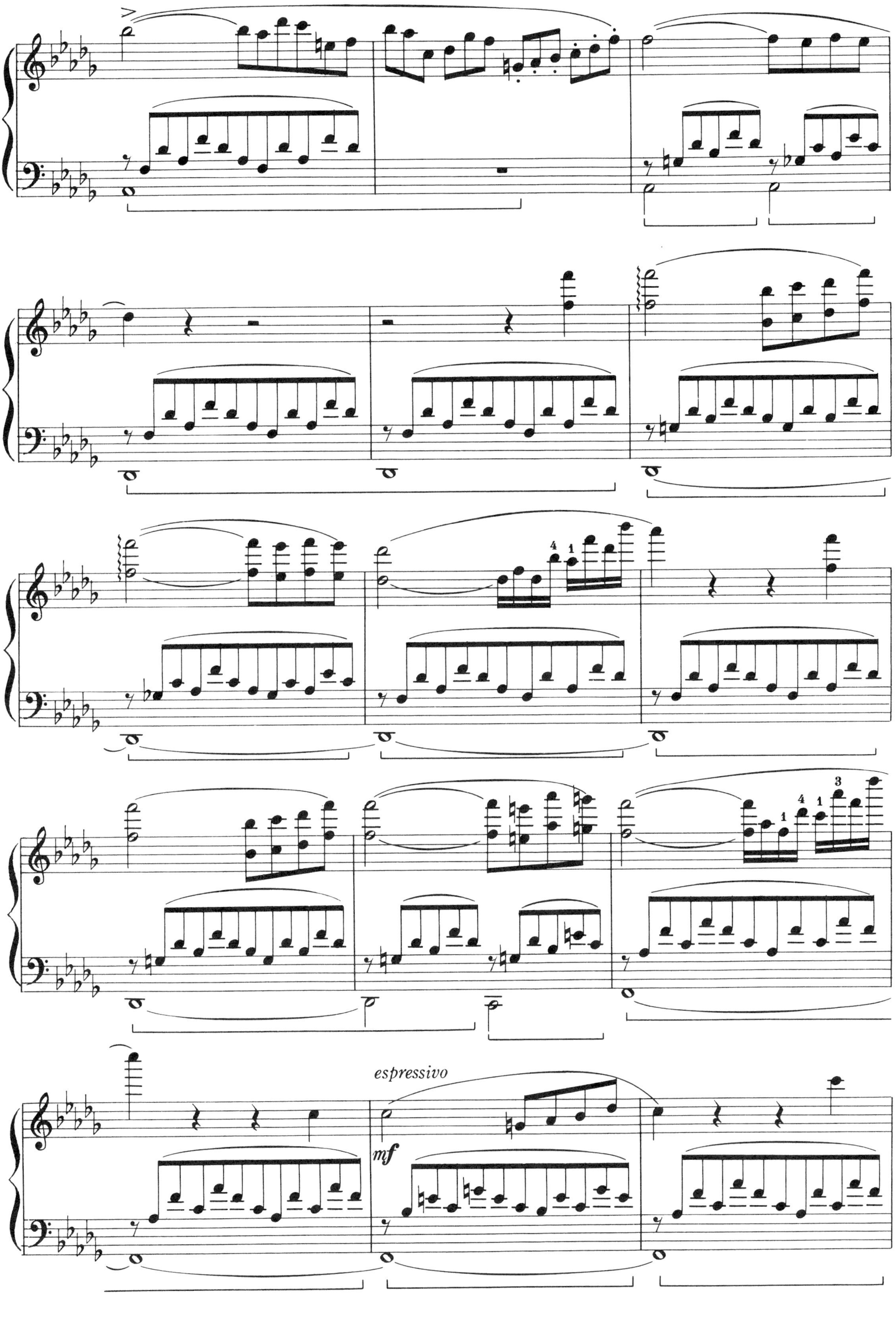
espressivo
mf

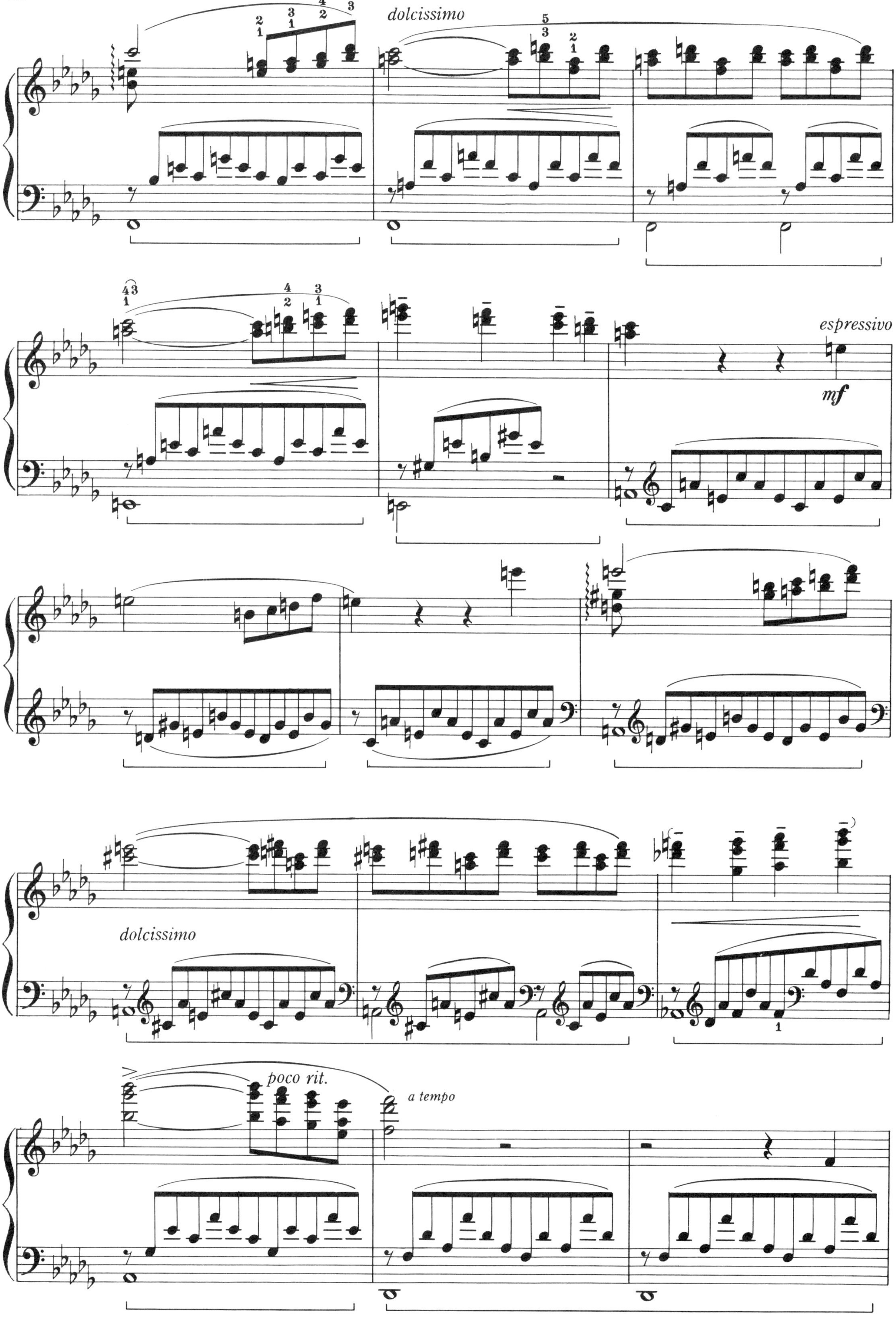
dolcissimo
espressivo
mf
dolcissimo
poco rit.
a tempo

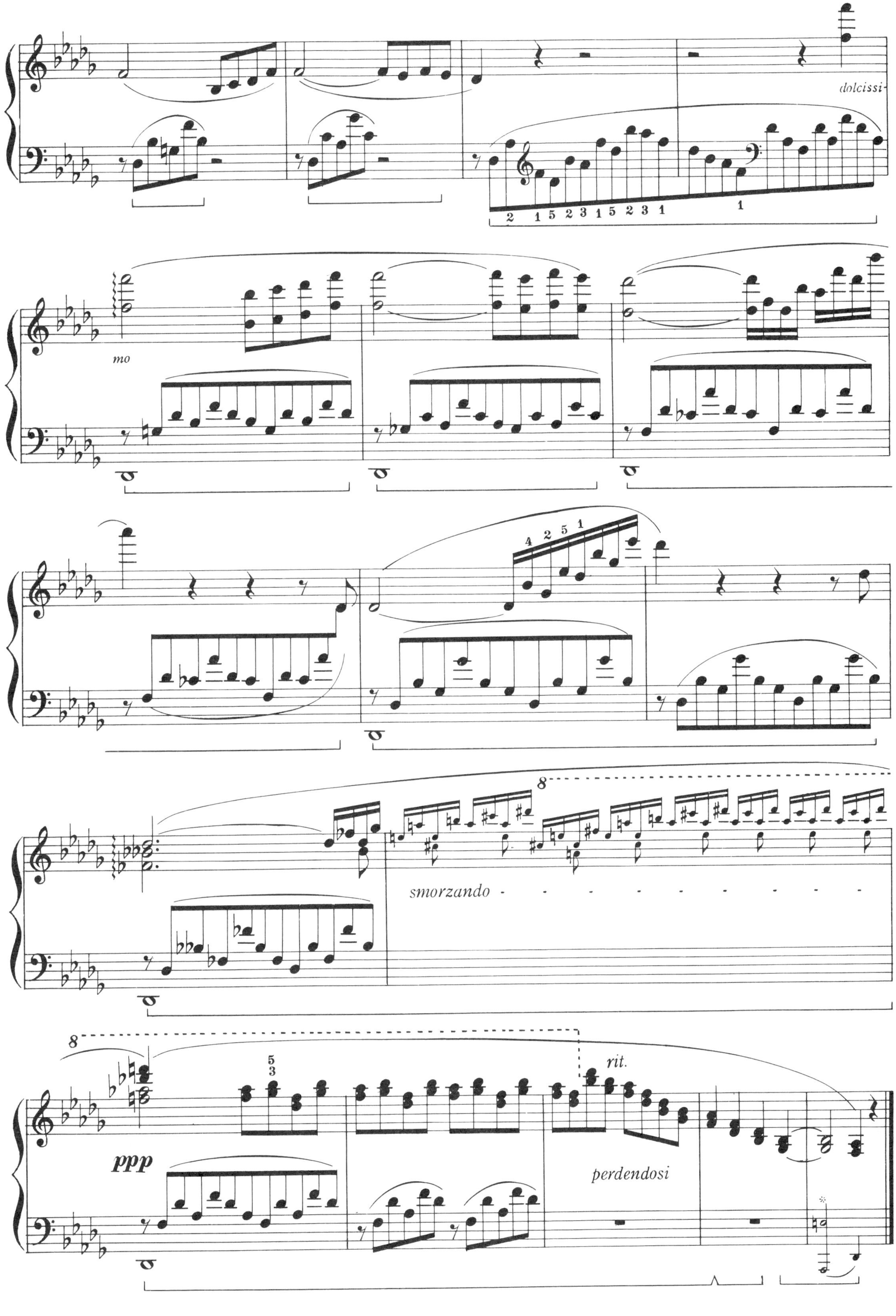
dolcissi-
mo
smorzando
8
ppp
rit.
perdendosi

CONSOLATION NO. 4

Franz Liszt
(1811-1886)

Quasi adagio

cantabile con divozione

marcato ed espressivo il basso
stringendo
dimin.
slargando
cresc.
Ped.

DANCE OF THE GNOMES

Franz Liszt
(1811-1886)

Un poco più animato

rinforzando
velocissimo
sf
Ped.
dimin.
p
pp
a tempo (come prima)
dim.
poco rallent.
pp

cresc.
Un poco più animato
rinforzando
p giocoso non legato
cresc.

più cresc.
Ped.
Ped. molto marcato
rinforzando velocissimo
sf
Ped.
dimin.
p leggiero
più dimin.
sempre presto e stacc.
pp
pp

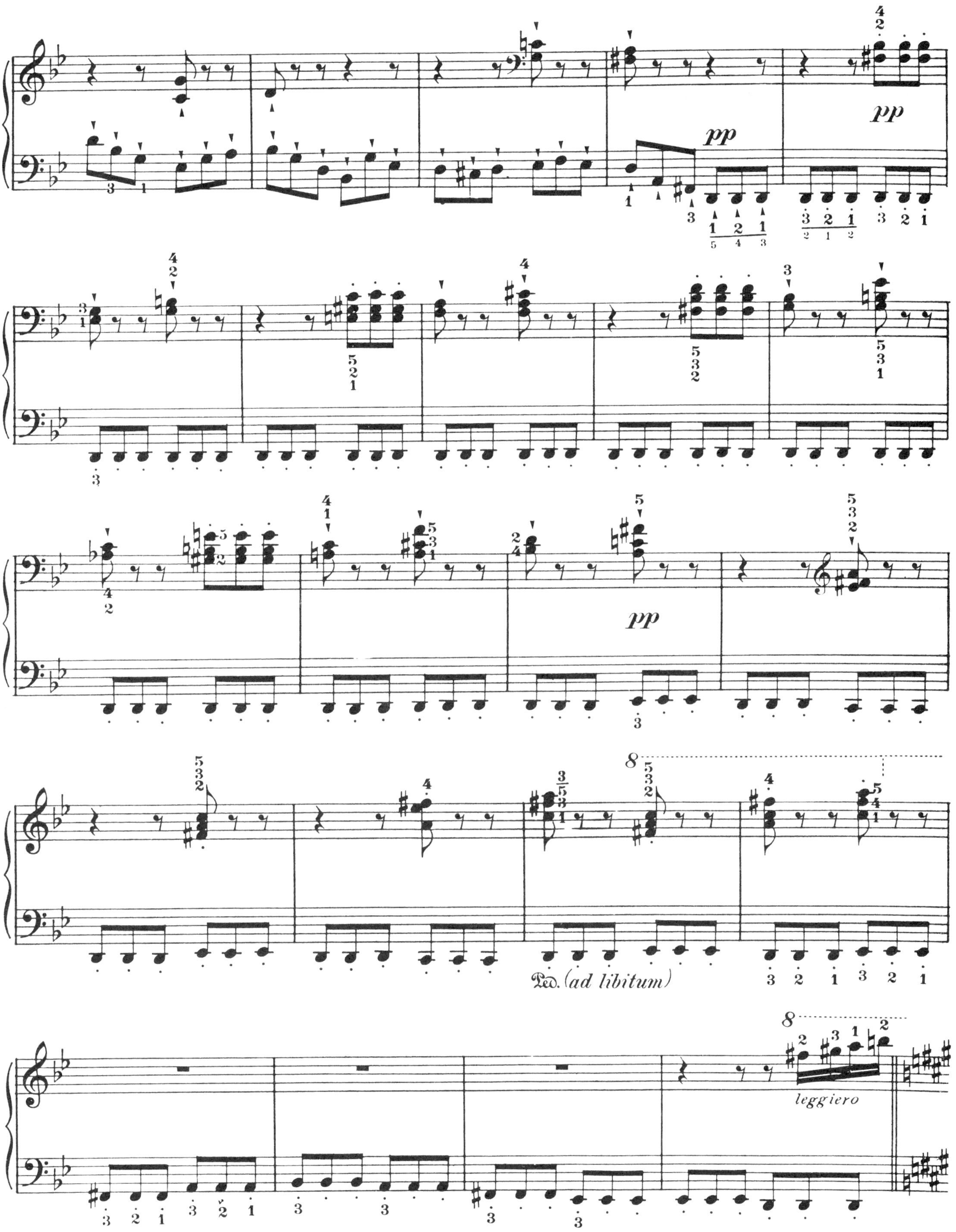
pp
pp
pp
Ped. (ad libitum)
leggiero

pp
sempre staccato
Ped.
sempre staccato
poco a poco cresc.
molto cresc. e string.
sf

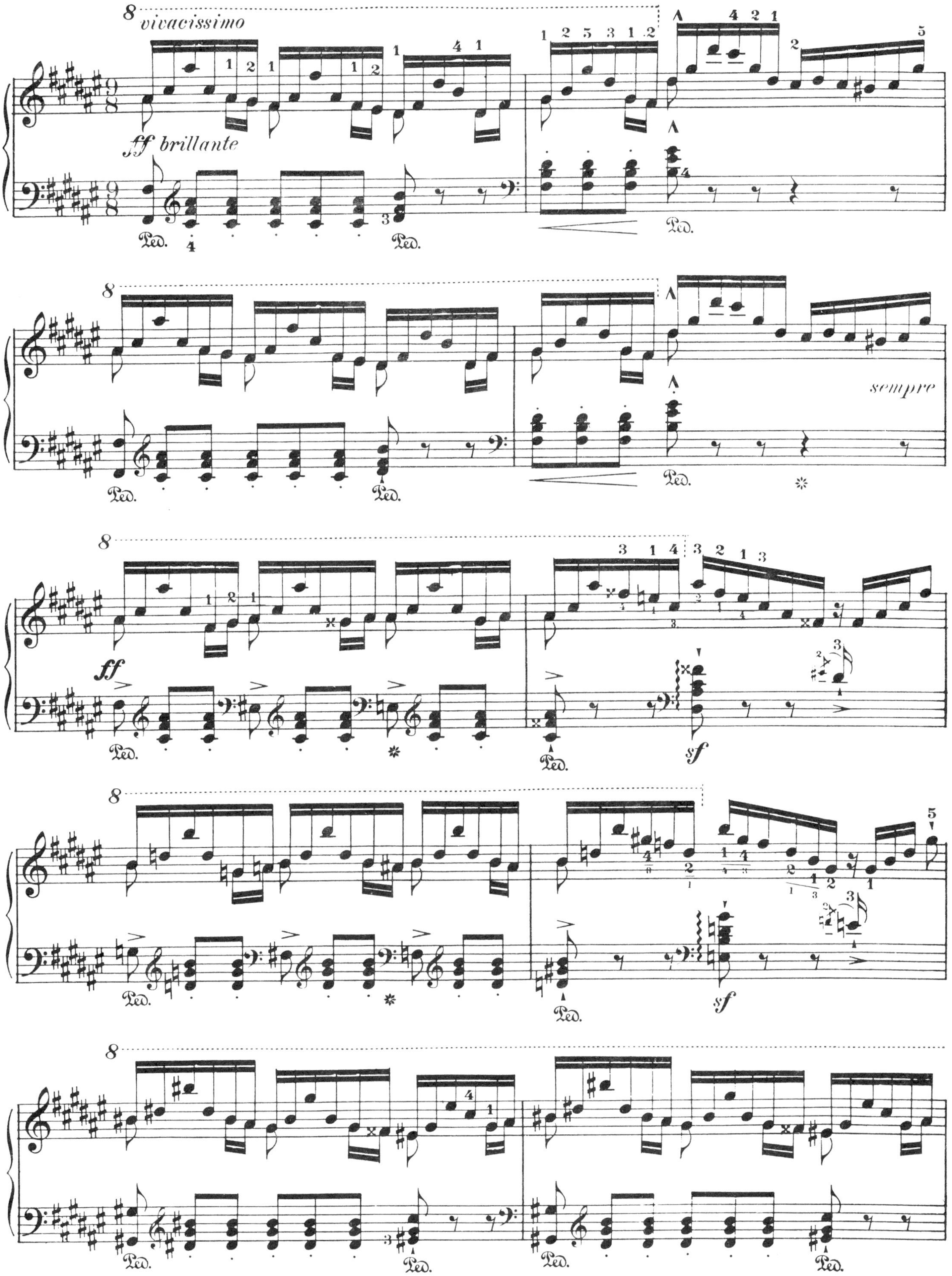
vivacissimo
ff brillante
sempre
ff
sf
sf

il più presto possibile e ff
marcato
marcato
rinforzando molto

p
sf
p sempre staccato
sempre più piano
ppp
staccato sempre
pp
pp
ppp
ppp

(The) ERL KING
(A Transcription of Schubert's Melody)

Franz Liszt
(1811-1886)

poco rf
poco rf
cresc.
OSSIA.
molto energico
pp
sotto voce ma marcato
f
pp
sempre marcato il canto
ansioso
mf
p
mf
pp

tranquillo
misterioso
ppp
espress.
legg.
precipitato
f
tre-
mante
rfz
p
dim.

tranquillo
pp un piu plus anime
legg. amorosamente
precipitato
tremante
rfz molto

dim.
p
Ped.
cresc.
ff
Ped.
p
pp
molto appassionato.
riten.
cresc. subito
OSSIA
ff
rfz

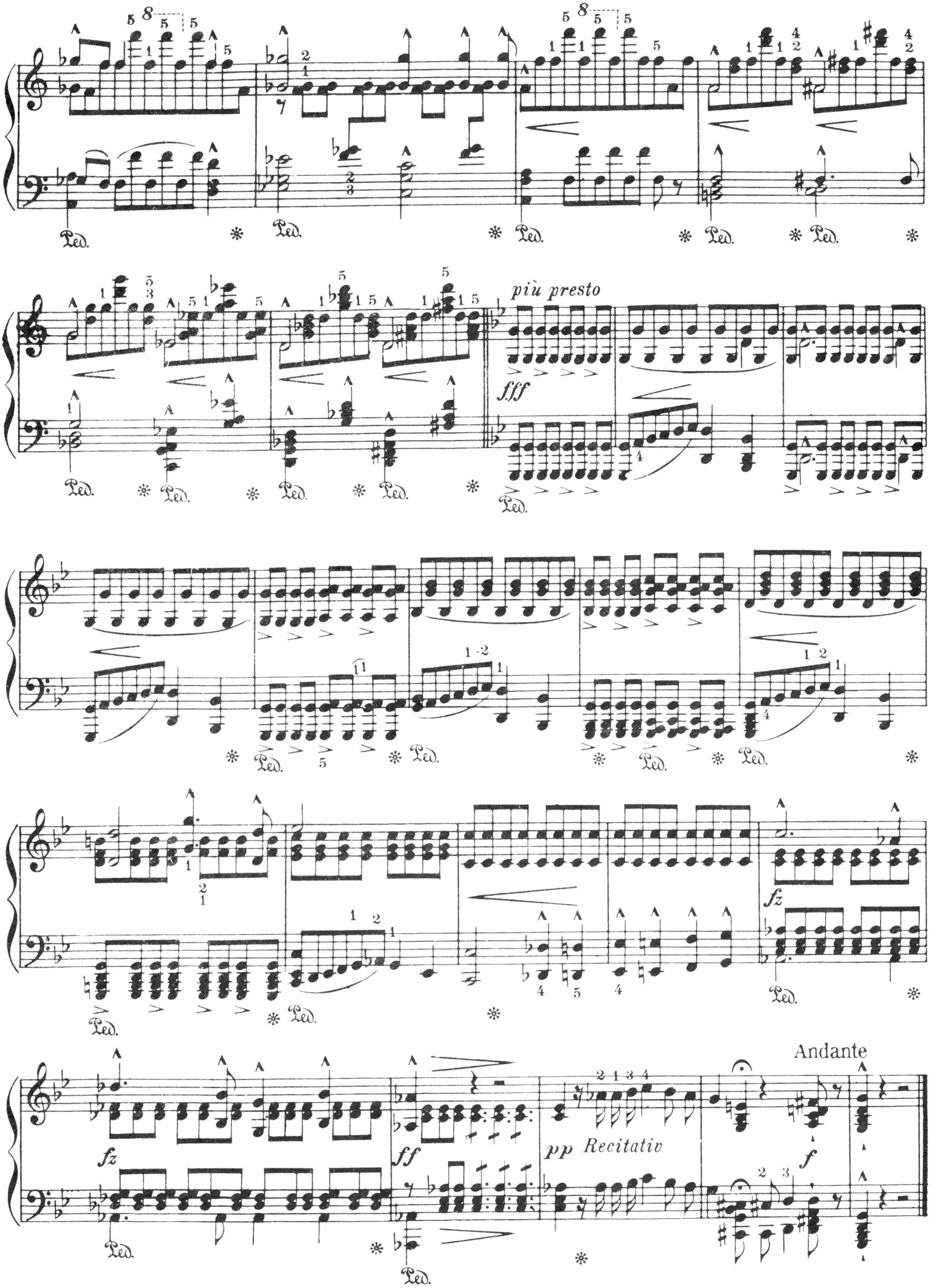
più presto
fff
fz
ff
pp Recitativ
f
Andante

ETUDE NO. 11
(Evening Harmonies)

Franz Liszt
(1811-1886)

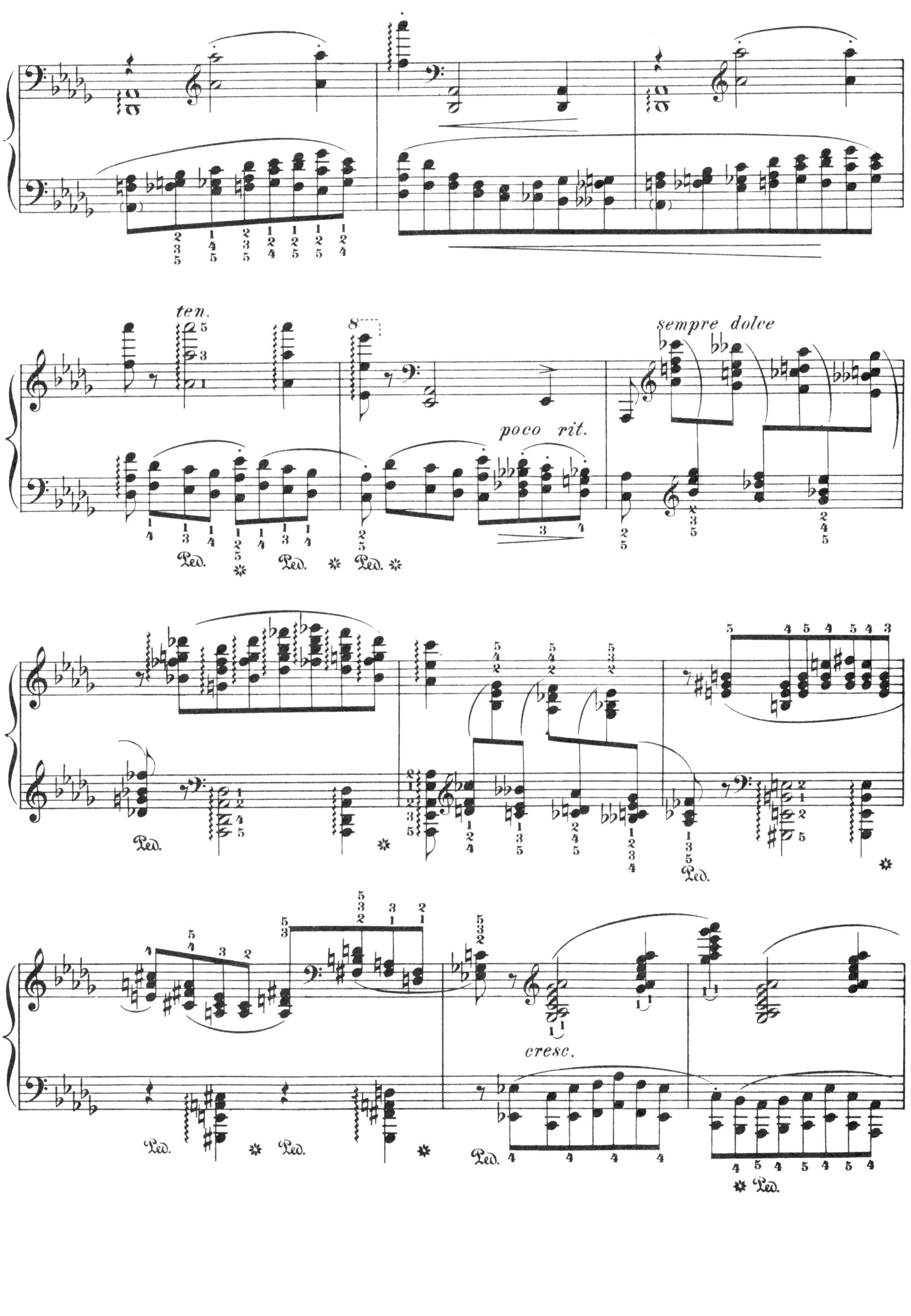
ten.
sempre dolce
poco rit.
Ped.
cresc.

un poco animato
più cresc.
sf
arpeggiato con molto sentimento
Ped.
(Pedal with each harmony)
Ped.
Ped.
Ped.
dimin.

Poco più mosso.
dolcissimo.

ppp *una corda*

ppp *sempre*

(tre corde)
cresc. -

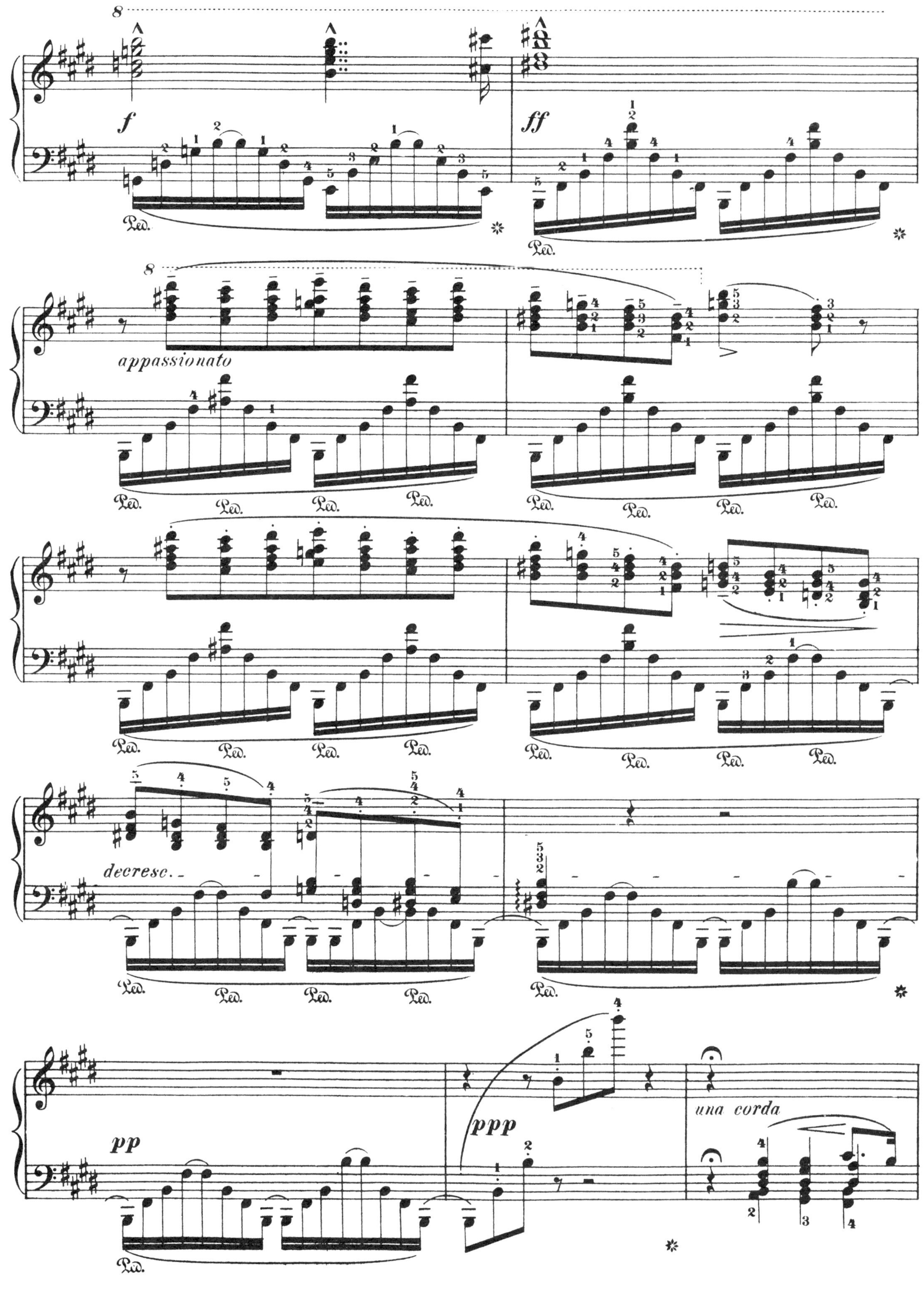

f
ff
Ped.
appassionato
decresc.
pp
ppp
una corda

Più lento con intimo sentimento.

accompagnamento quasi Arpa.

rinforz.

(tre corde)

ff

rinforz.

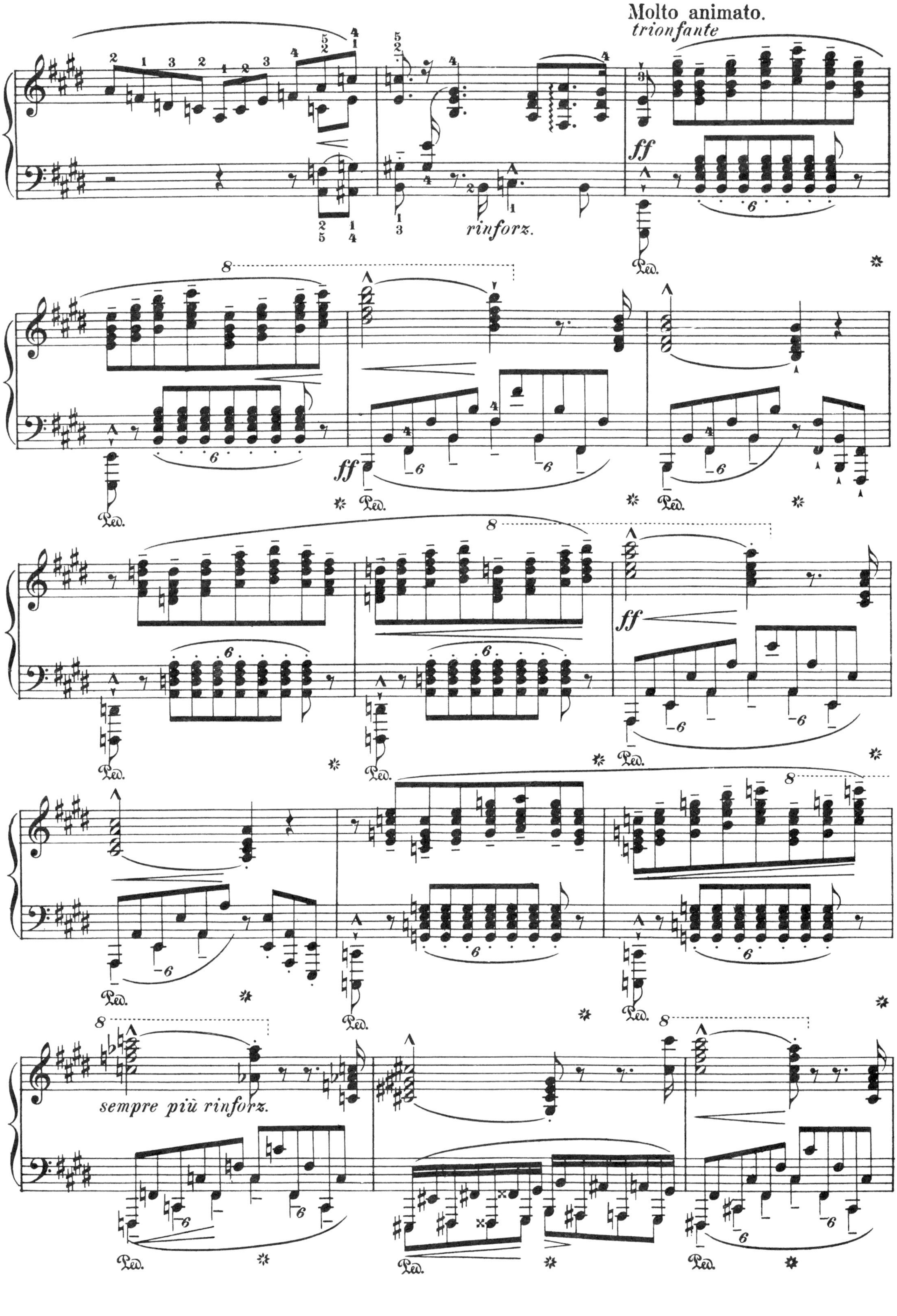
Molto animato.
trionfante
ff
rinforz.
Ped.
sempre più rinforz.

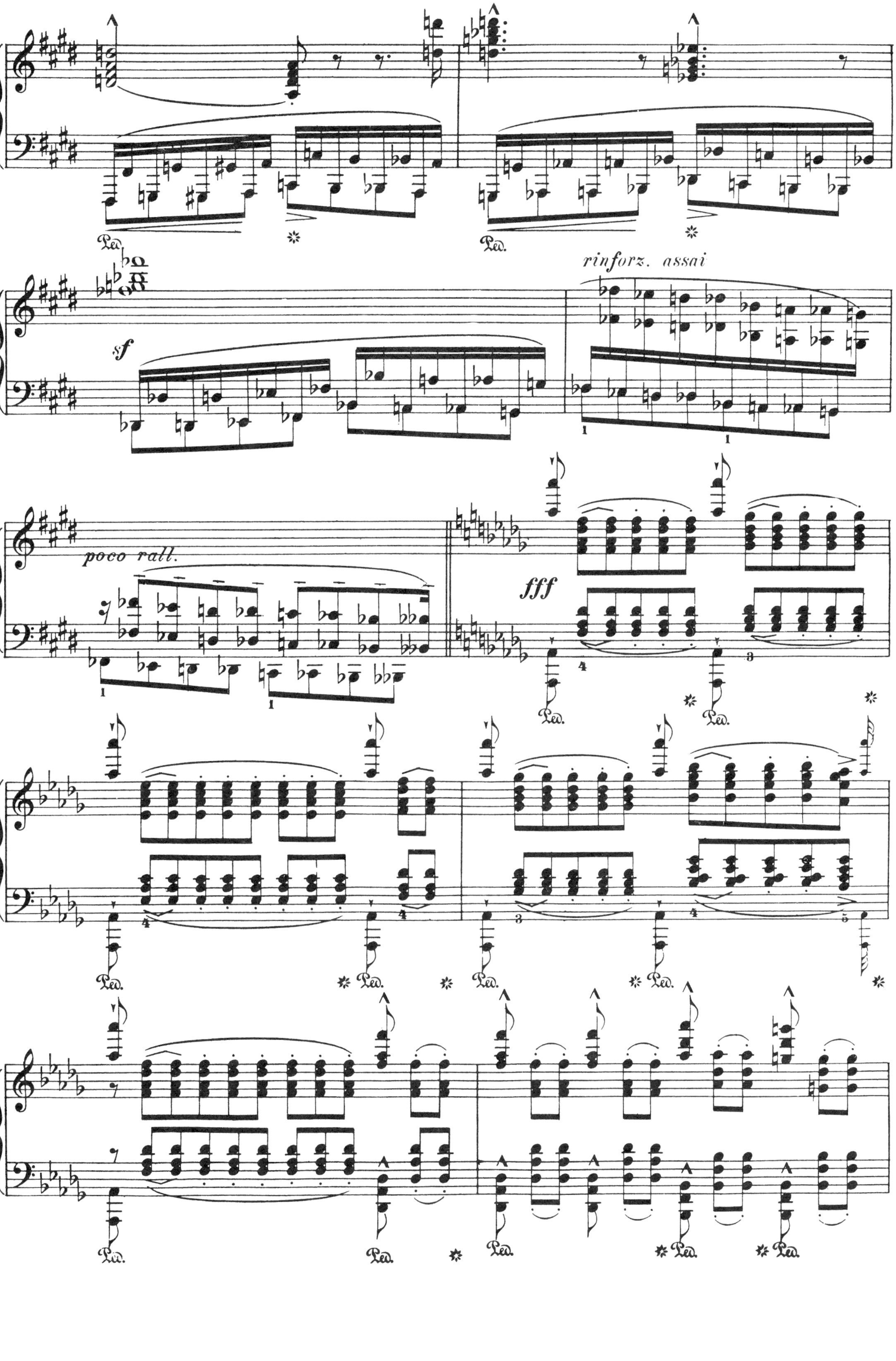

sf
rinforz. assai
poco rall.
fff
Ped.

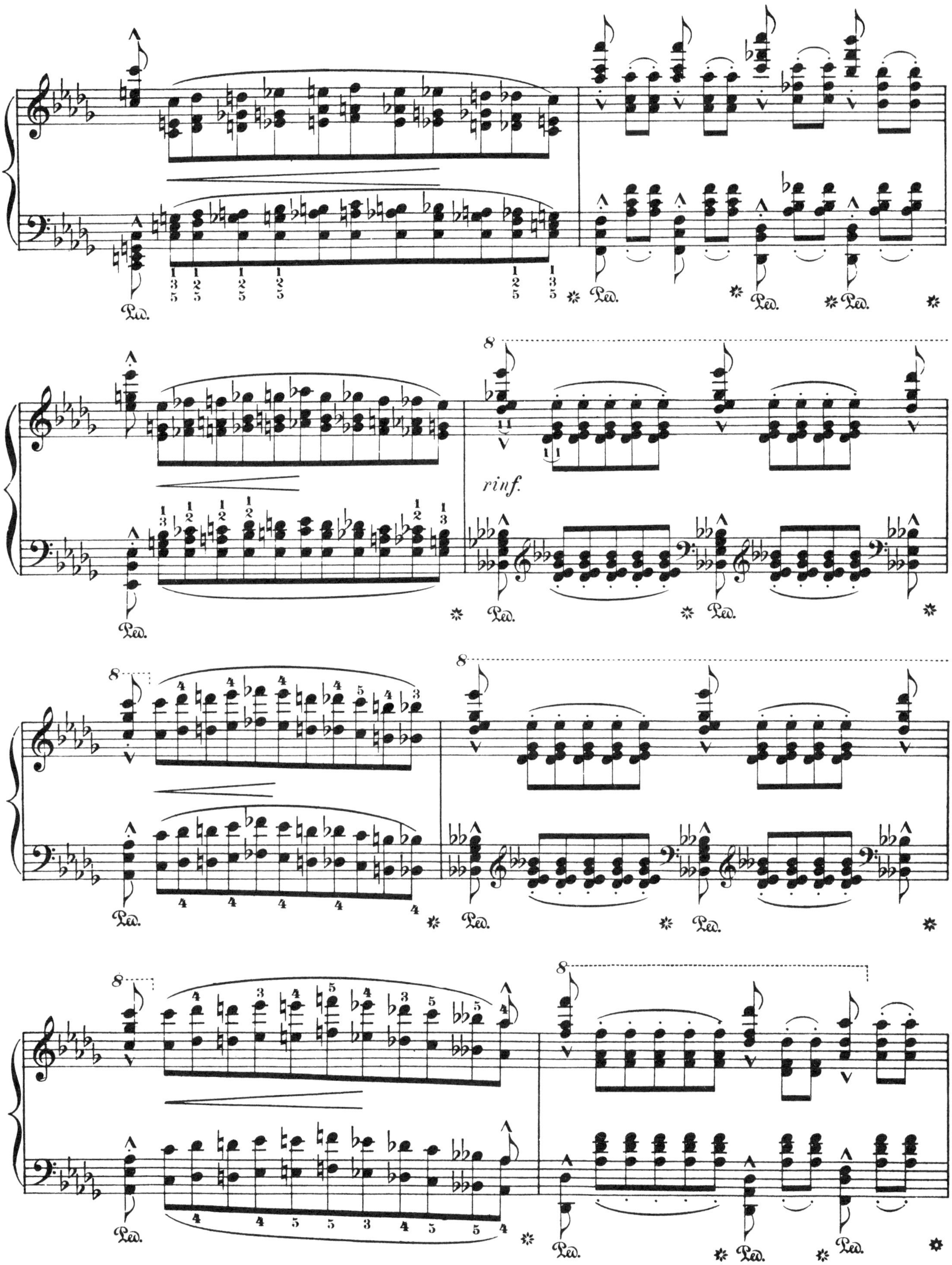
rinf.
Ped.

Ped.
sf
(sempre Ped.)
rinforz.
poco ritenuto
fff
Più animato
sempre fff

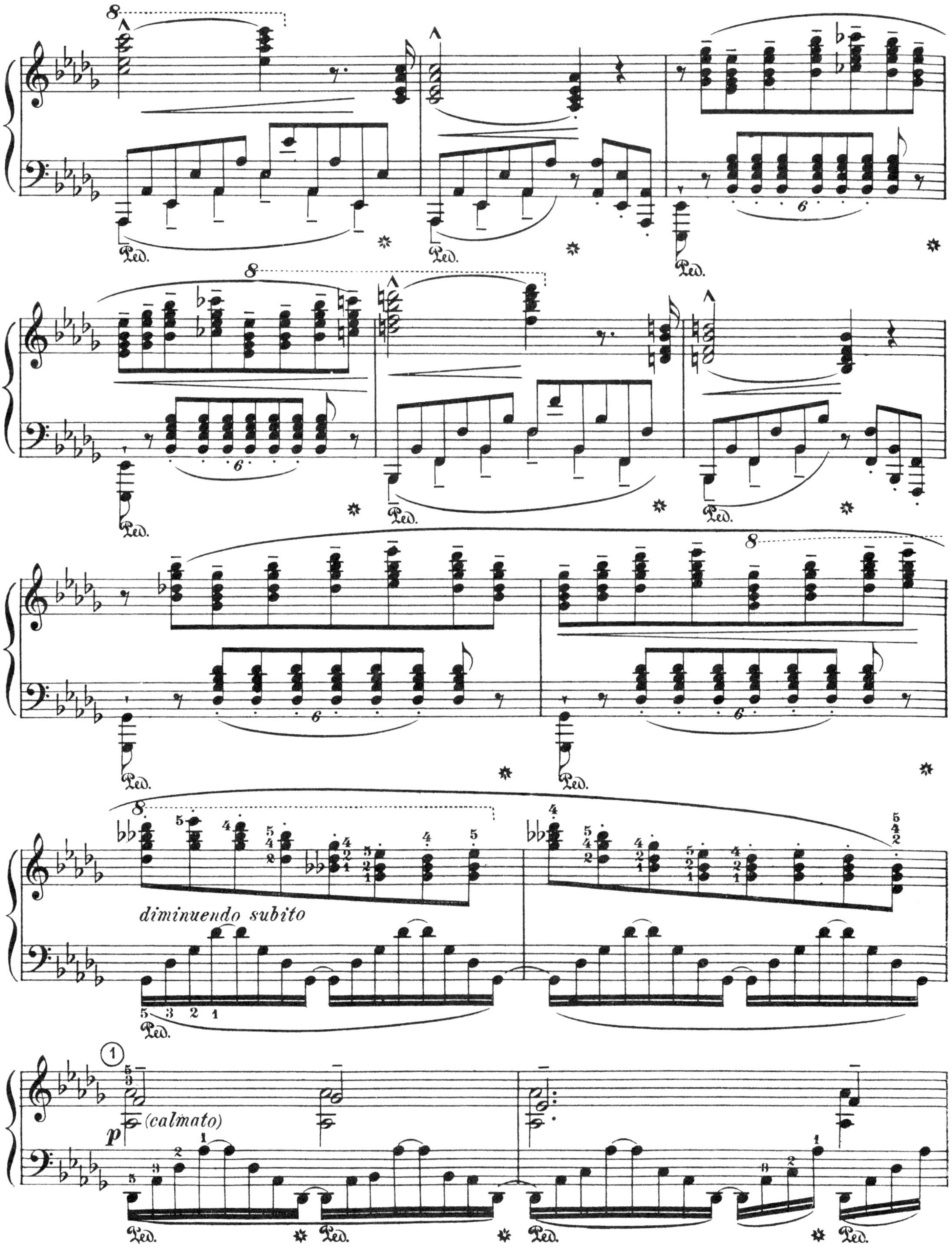
diminuendo subito
(calmato)
Ped.

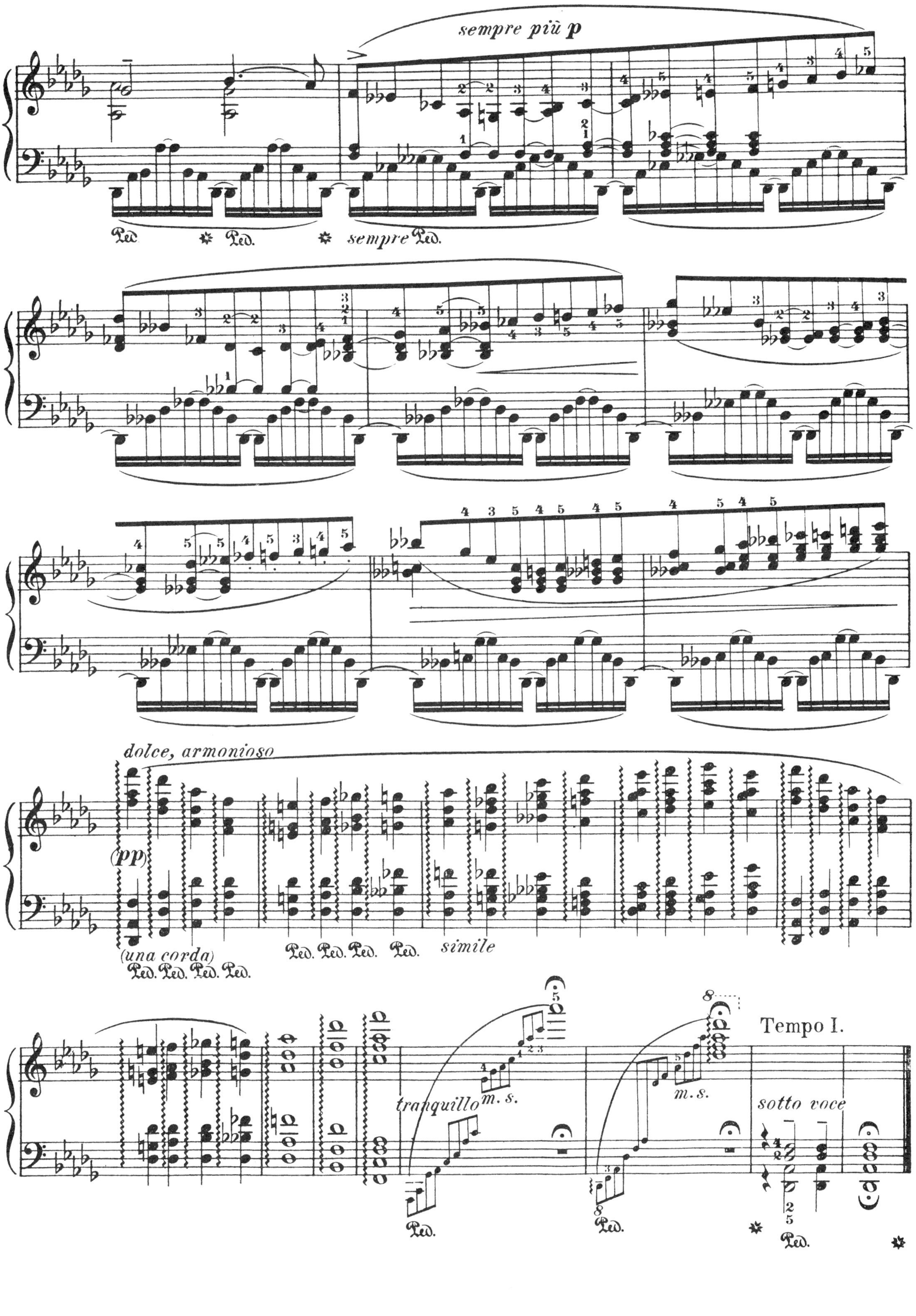
sempre più p
Ped.
Ped.
sempre Ped.
dolce, armonioso
(pp)
(una corda)
Ped. Ped. Ped. Ped.
Ped. Ped. Ped. Ped.
simile
tranquillo
m. s.
m. s.
Tempo I.
sotto voce
Ped.
Ped.
Ped.

ETUDE IN E
(From the Suite "Years of Pilgrimage")

Franz Liszt
(1811-1886)

poco a
poco
cresc.
ed
accelerando
8
molto
rinforz.
rit.
ff
Andante quieto
dolce
smorz.

Più lento
una corda
ppp
dolcissimo
Ped.
l.h.
un poco
sotto voce
marcato e rallentando a piacere
cresc.
stringendo

molto   rinforz.   ed appassionato

Quasi allegretto mosso

ff

dolce armonioso

legato

con grazia

pp

creso.

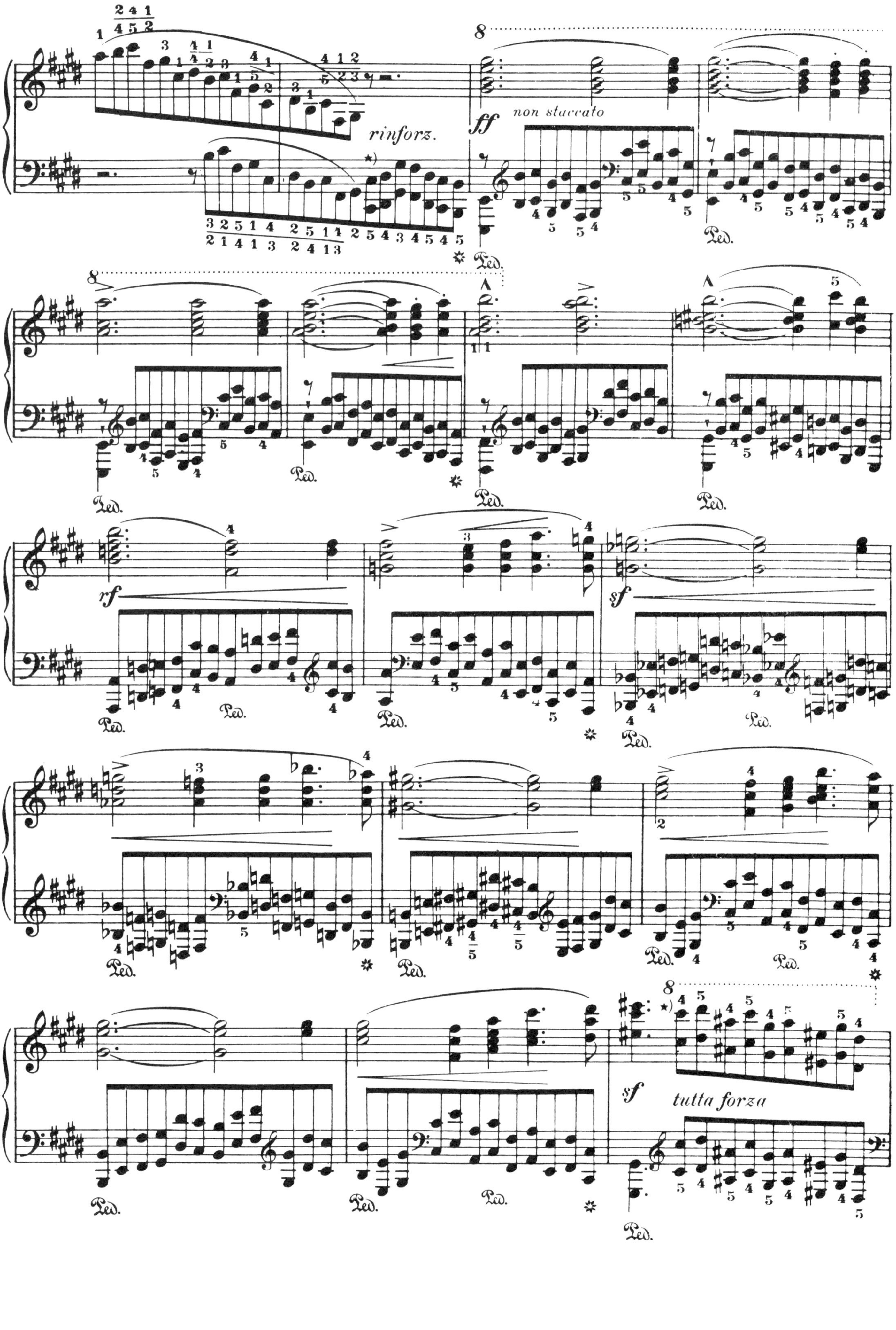
rinforz.
ff
non staccato
rf
sf
sf
tutta forza

fff
Ped.
ritenuto il tempo
dolce
dolce
pp
pp
poco a poco ritenuto
Adagio
e smorzando
ppp

FAREWELL
(Abscheid)

Franz Liszt
(1811-1886)

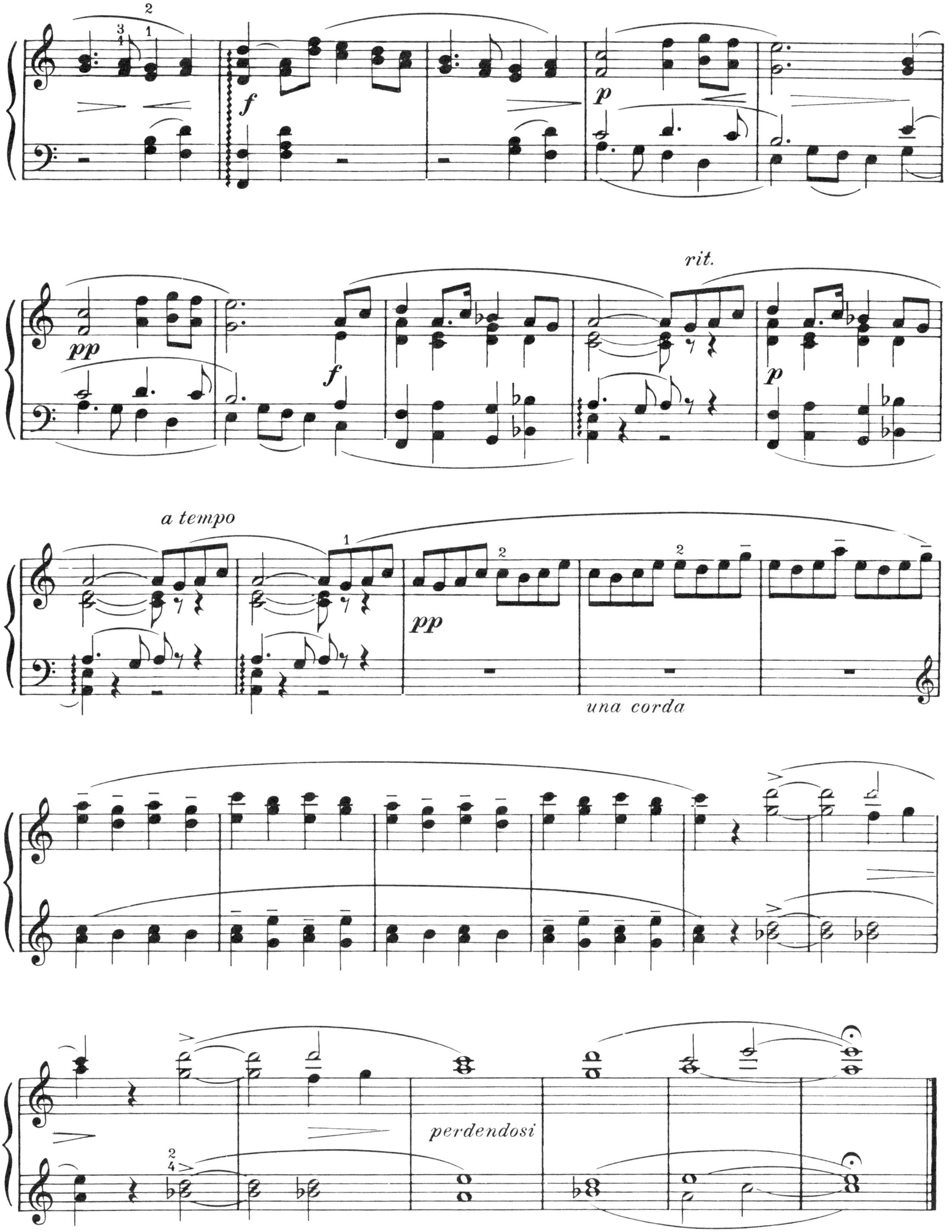
rit.
a tempo
una corda
perdendosi

FUNERAL PROCESSION OF GONDOLAS
NO. 1

Franz Liszt
(1811-1886)

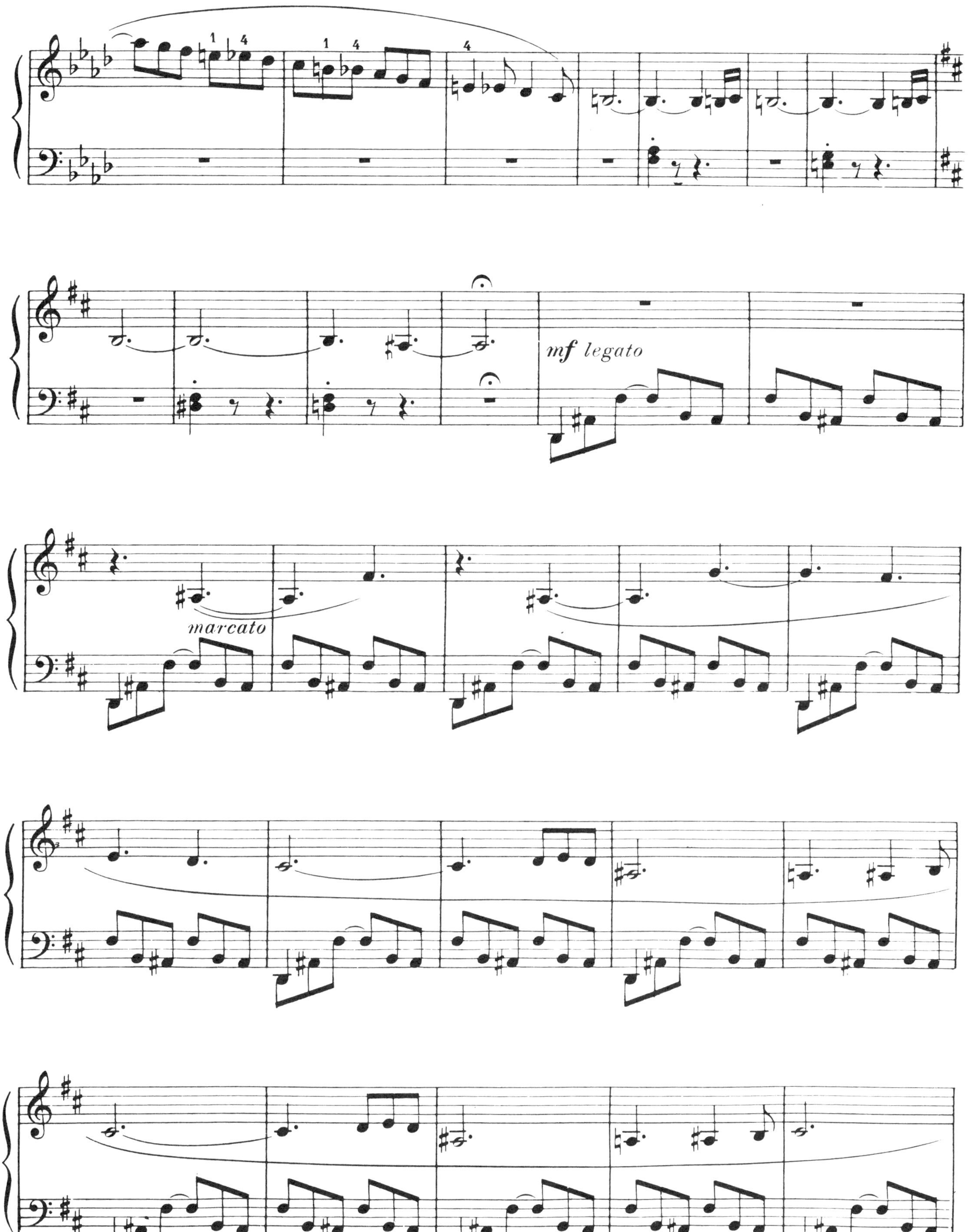
mf legato
marcato

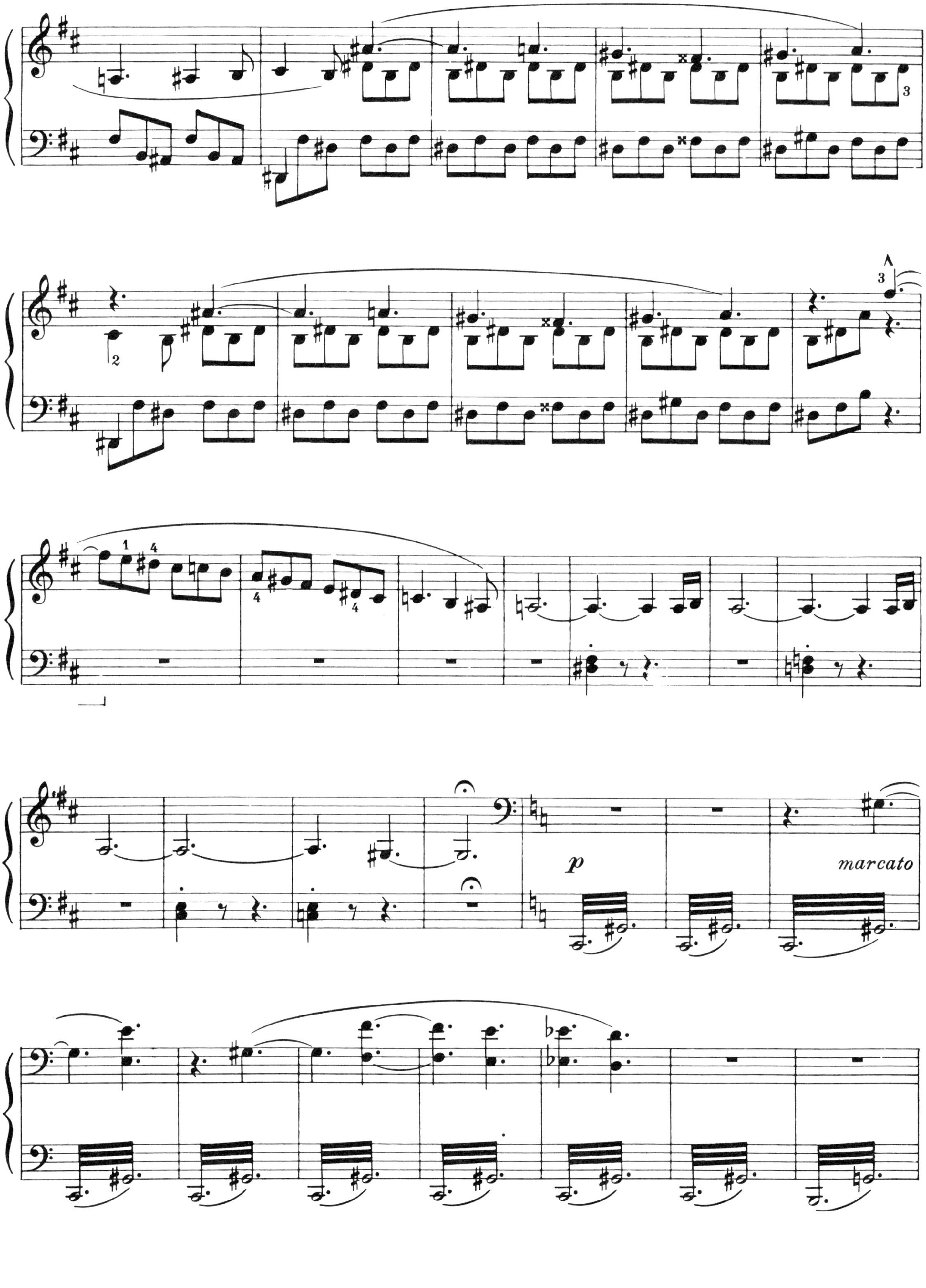
p
marcato

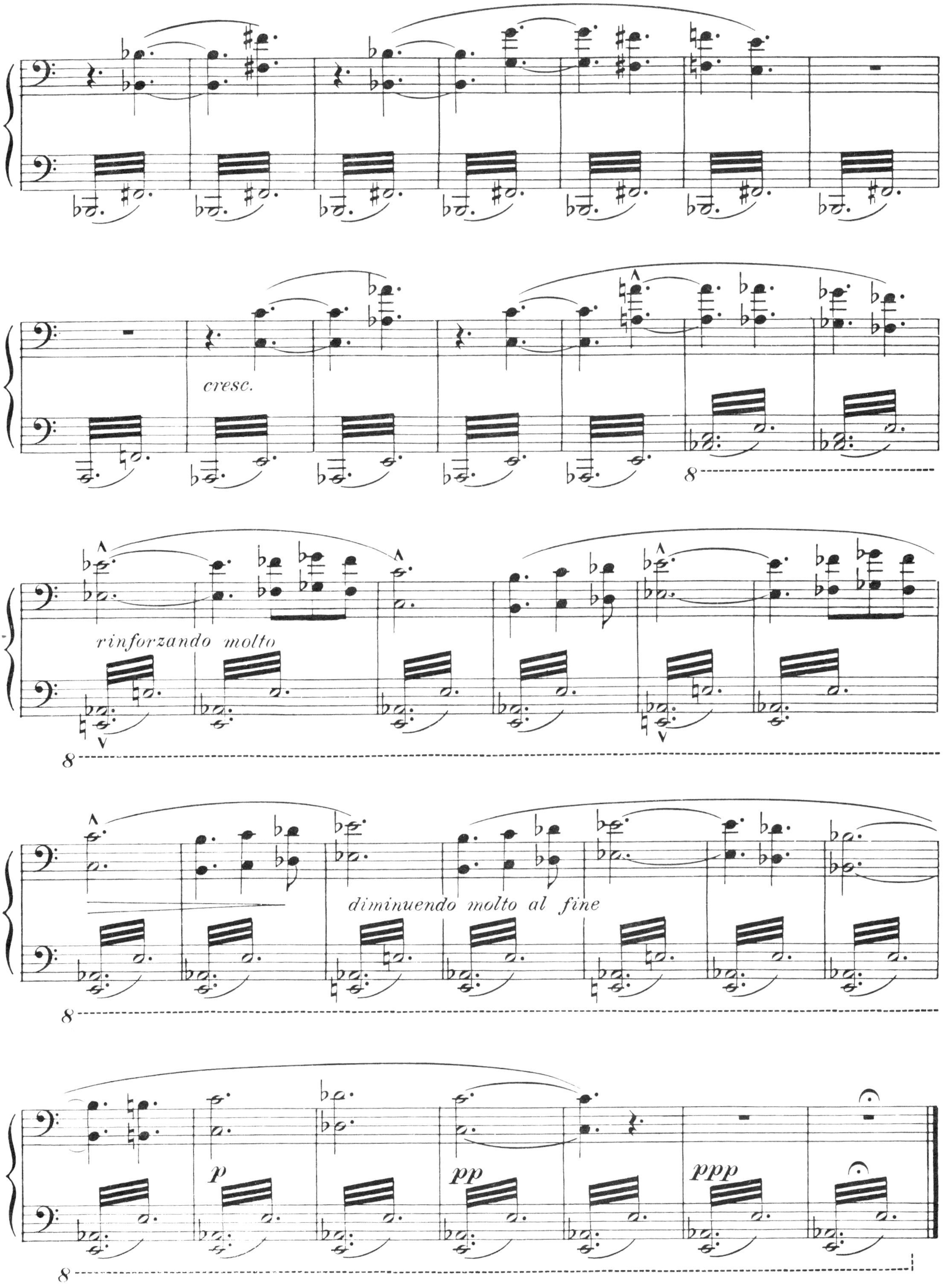
cresc.
rinforzando molto
diminuendo molto al fine
p
pp
ppp

FUNERAL PROCESSION OF GONDOLAS
NO.2

Andante mesto, non troppo lento ♩=88

Franz Liszt
(1811-1886)

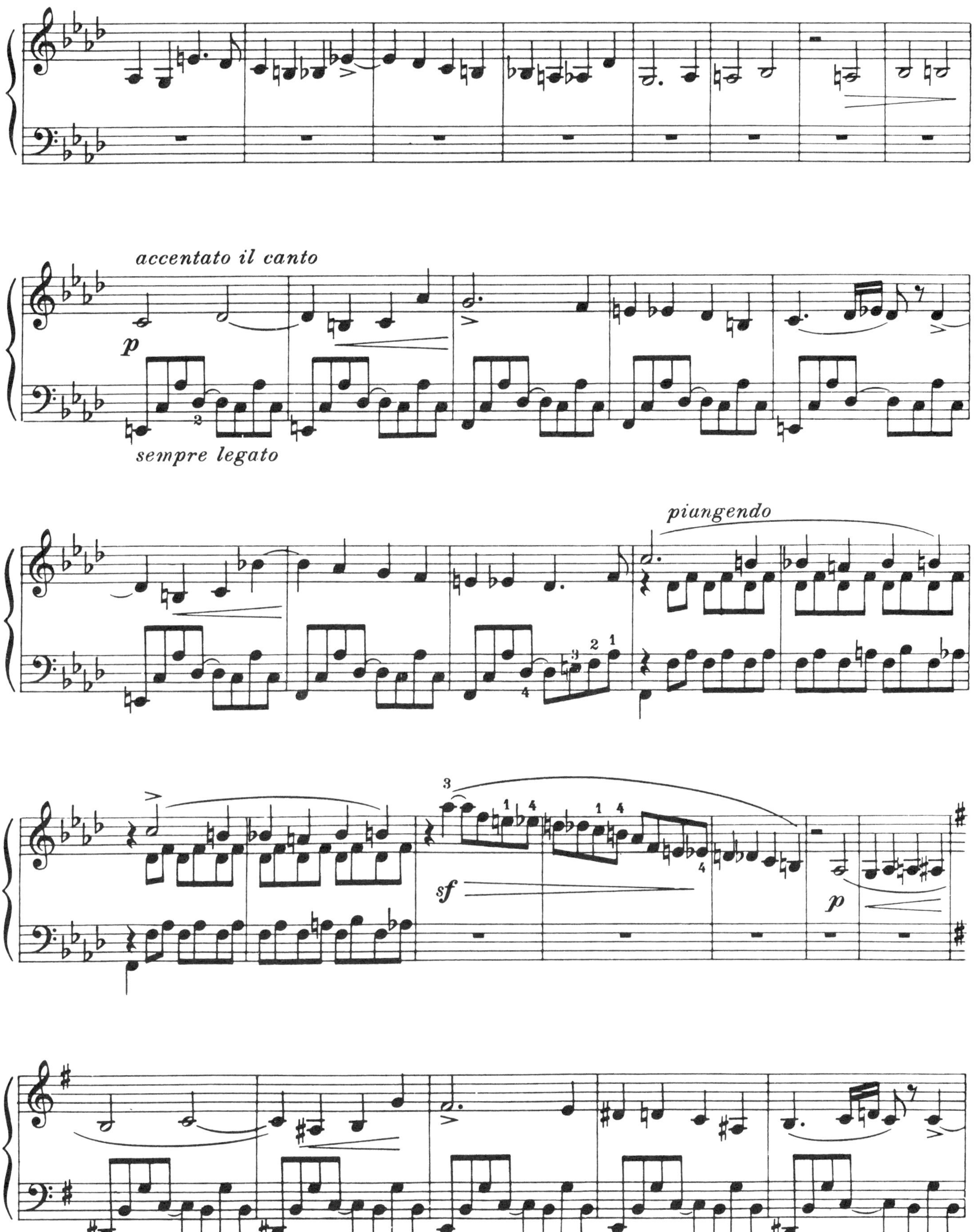
accentato il canto
p
sempre legato
piangendo
sf
p

piangendo
sf
p
Un poco meno lento ♩= 104
dolcissimo, dolente
sempre legato

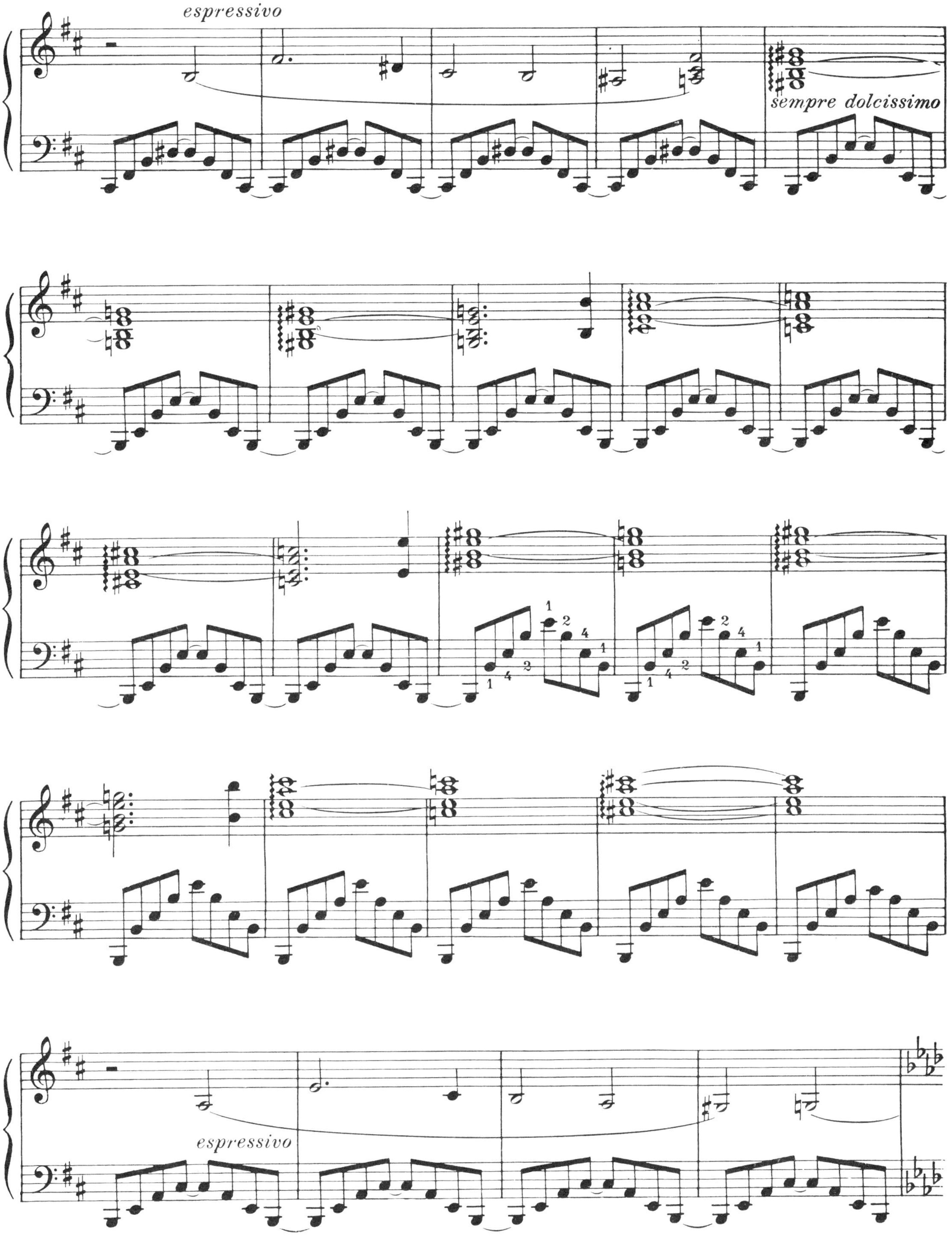
espressivo
sempre dolcissimo
espressivo

appassionato
mf
rinforzando
ff
fff legato
ff
dim.
recitando
mp

dim. molto
accentato
un poco ritenuto
mf pesante
5
5
pp
mf
ritenuto
pp

HUNGARIAN RHAPSODY NO. 2

Franz Liszt
(1811-1886)

Lento ed a capriccio

LASSAN.

Andante mesto.

capriccio
dolcissimo
ten.
ten.
ten.
ten.
sempre pp e leggierissimo
p giocoso

poco dim.
pp
cresc. molto
come prima
rit.
a tempo
espressivo assai
ritenuto
sf
l.h.
r.h.
accelerando

crescendo molto
rinforzando
diminuendo molto
espressivo
p dolce
rfz
dim.
p
dim.
rit.
lunga pausa.
un poco marcato e rall.
morendo

FRISKA.

Vivace.

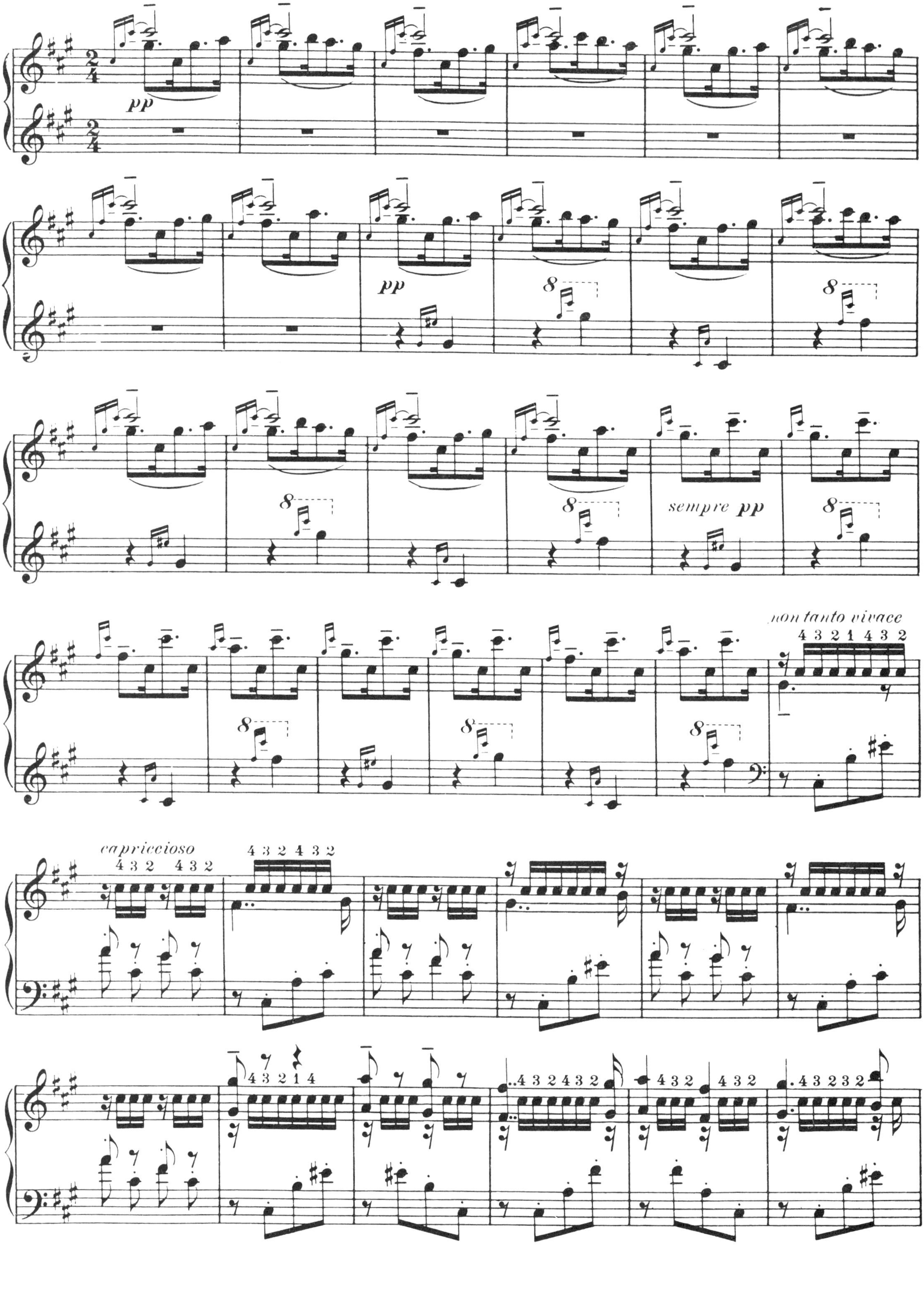

poco a poco accel. e cresc.
1 2 1
cresc. molto
Tempo giusto-vivace.
f marcato assai
p scherzando
4 5
il basso sempre staccato

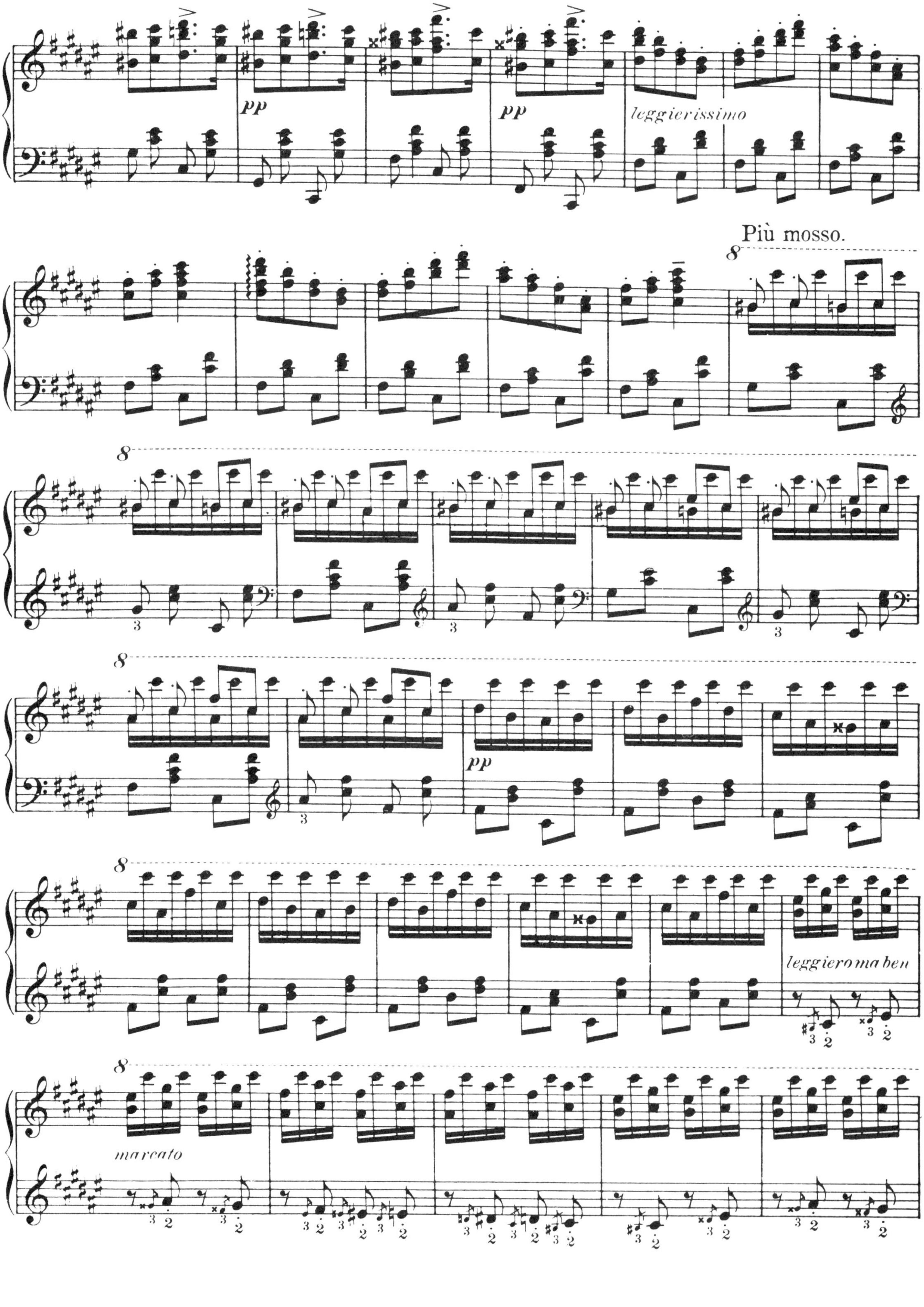
pp
pp
leggierissimo
Più mosso.
8
pp
leggiero ma ben
marcato

marcato
p sempre e poco a poco accelerando il tempo
sf
sf
sf
sf

stringendo e strepitoso
a tempo
sf
fff
brioso assai
tutta forza e stringendo
dim - in - u - en - do

8
p accelerando
pp
8
mp ma ben marcato
senza pedale
pp
p e sempre staccato
p e sempre staccato
8

Ossia.
crescendo molto
stringendo
sfz
a tempo
sf
brioso assai
fff
sf
sf
sf
tutta forza

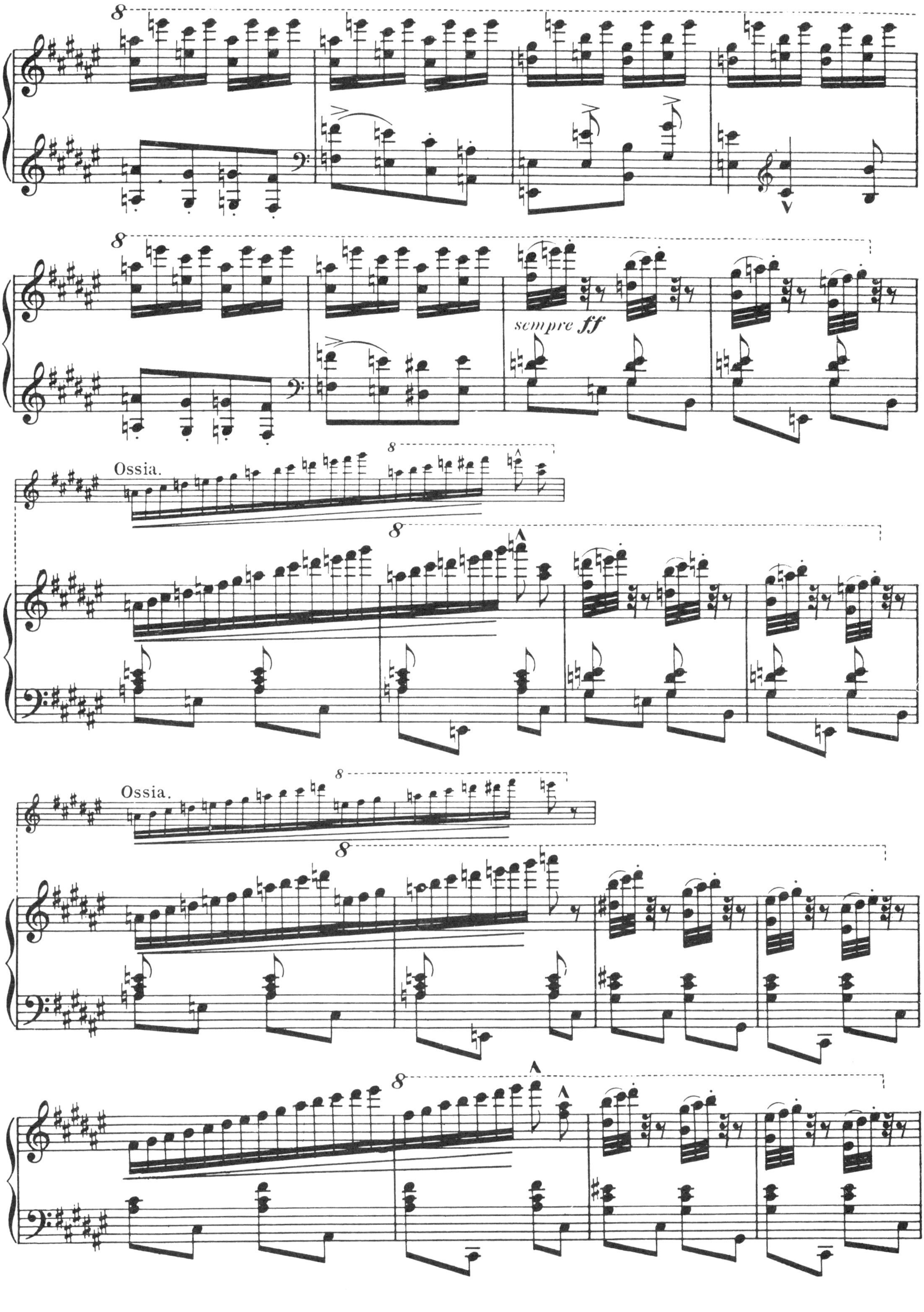
sempre ff
Ossia.
Ossia.

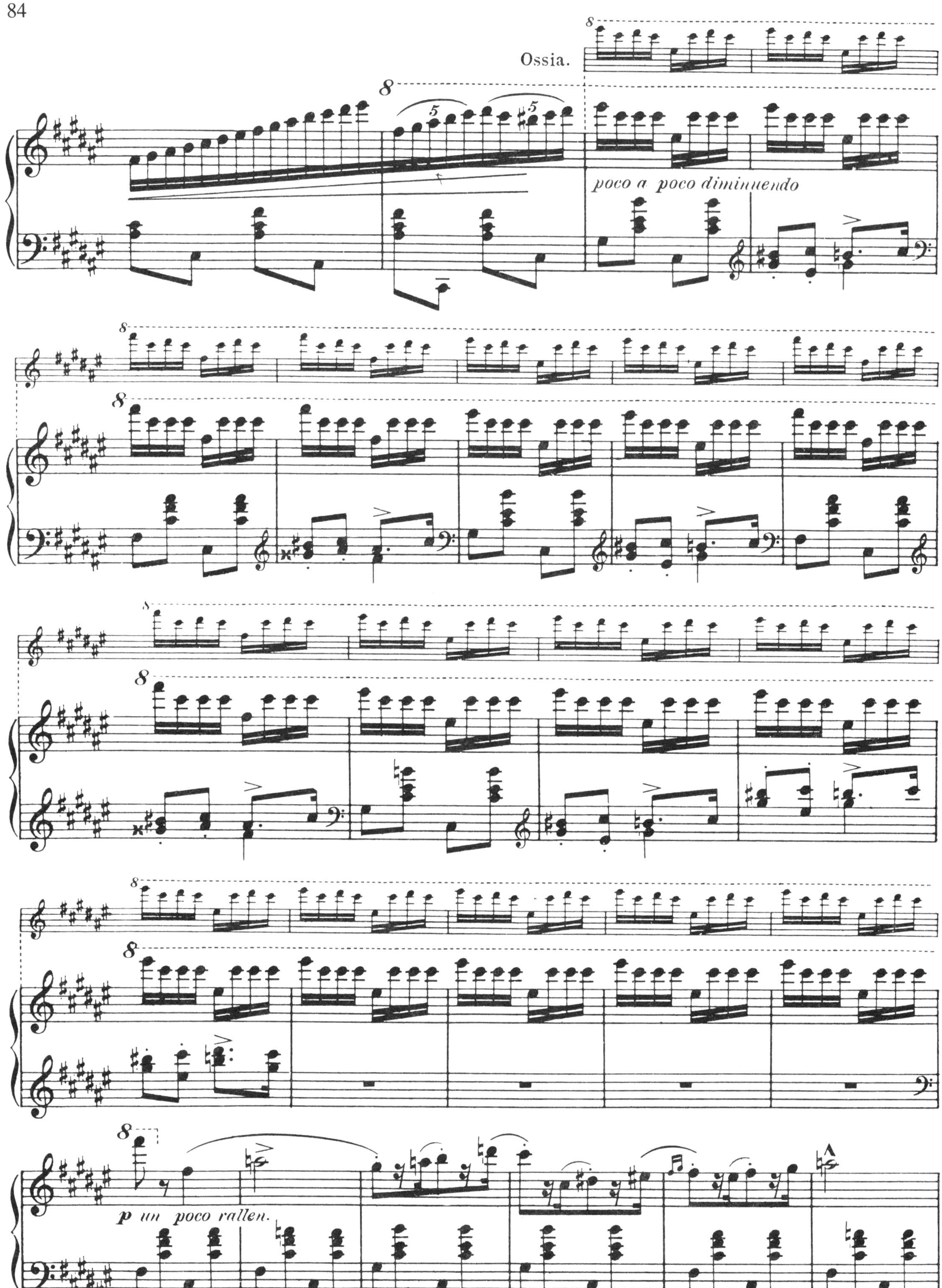

Ossia.
poco a poco diminuendo
p un poco rallen.

Cadenza ad lib.
più ritenuto
Prestissimo.
pp martellato
cresc.
più cresc.
8
ff
Presto.

HUNGARIAN RHAPSODY NO. 6

Franz Liszt
(1811-1886)

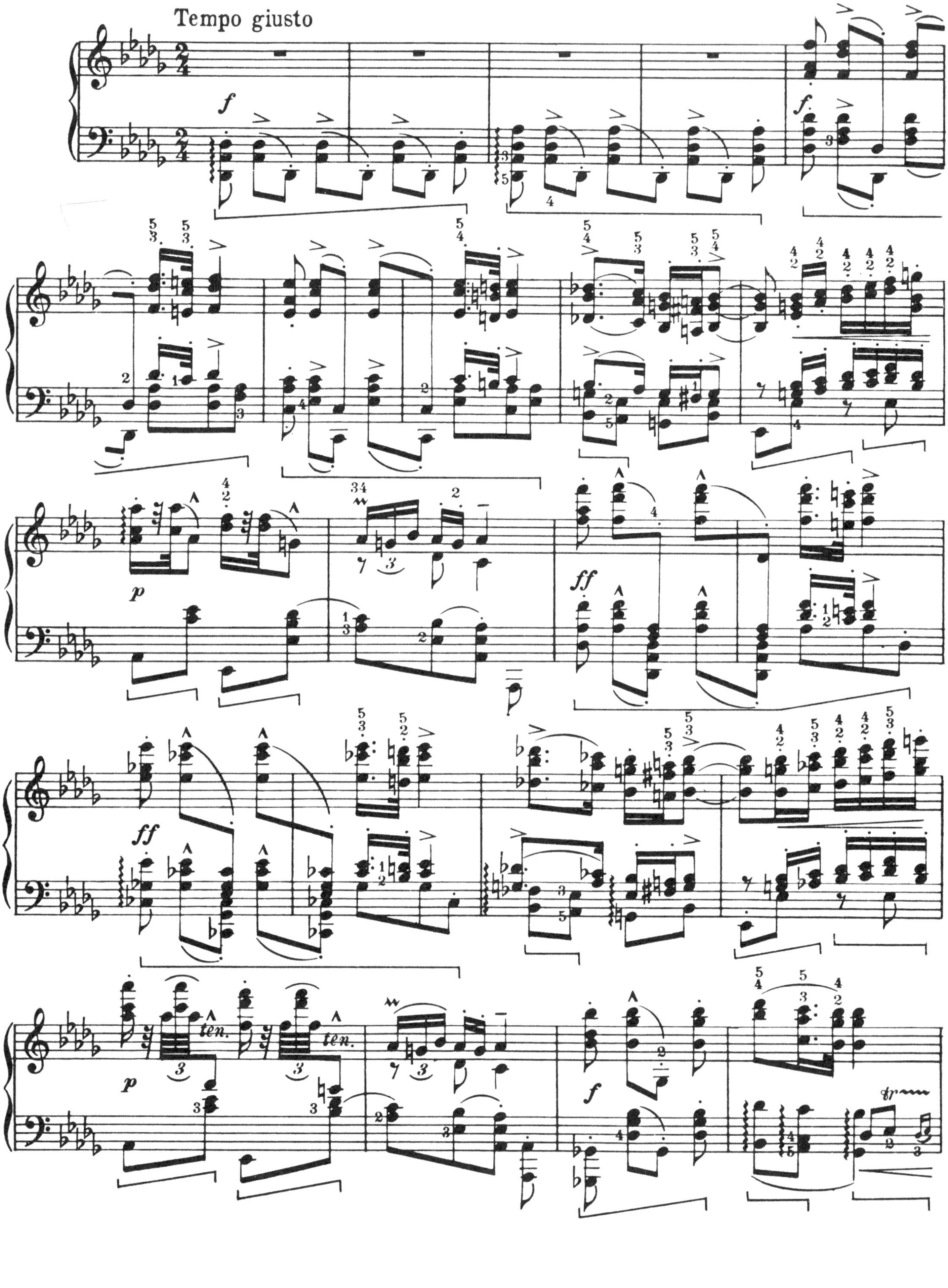

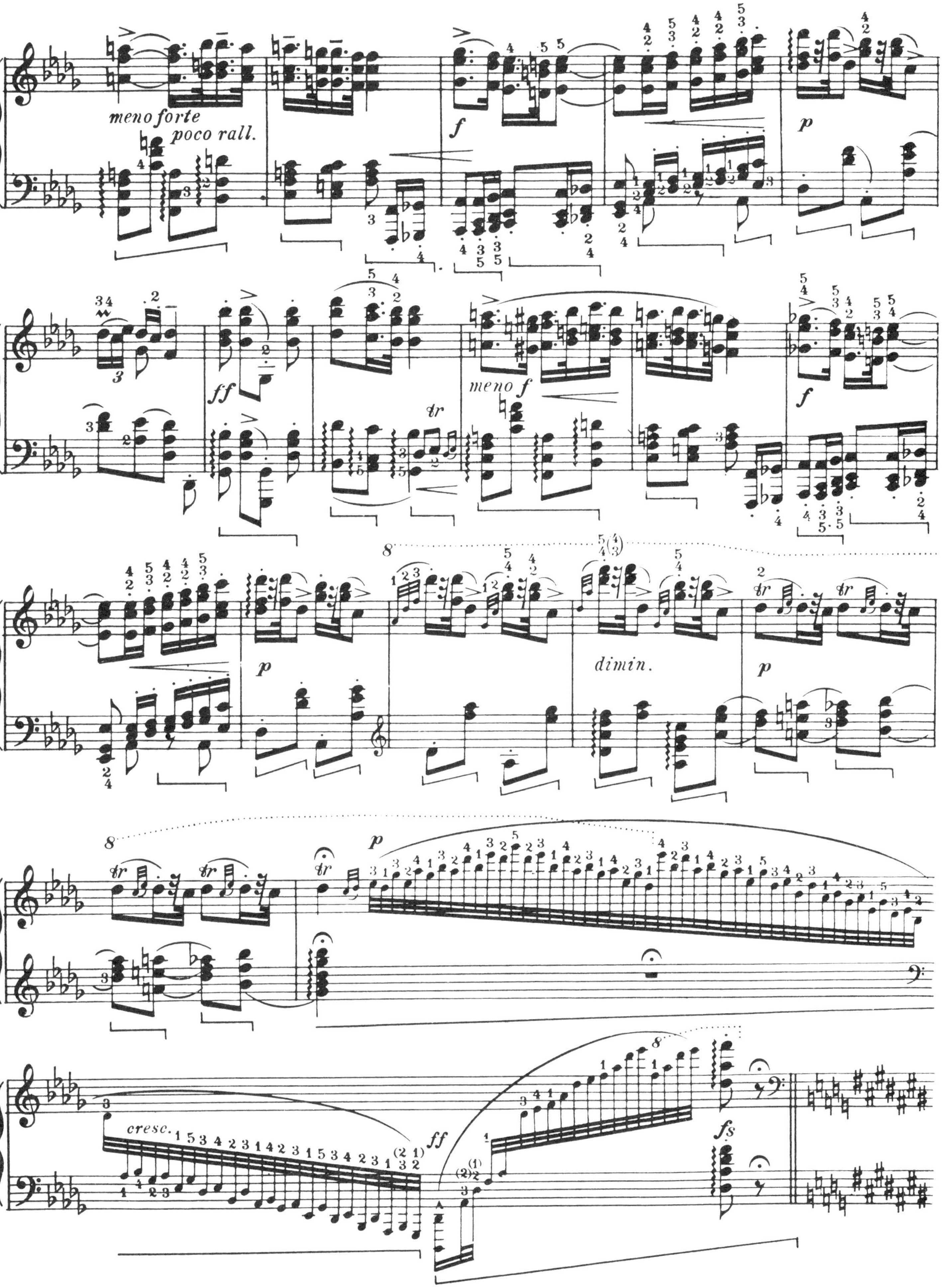
meno forte
poco rall.
meno f
dimin.
cresc.

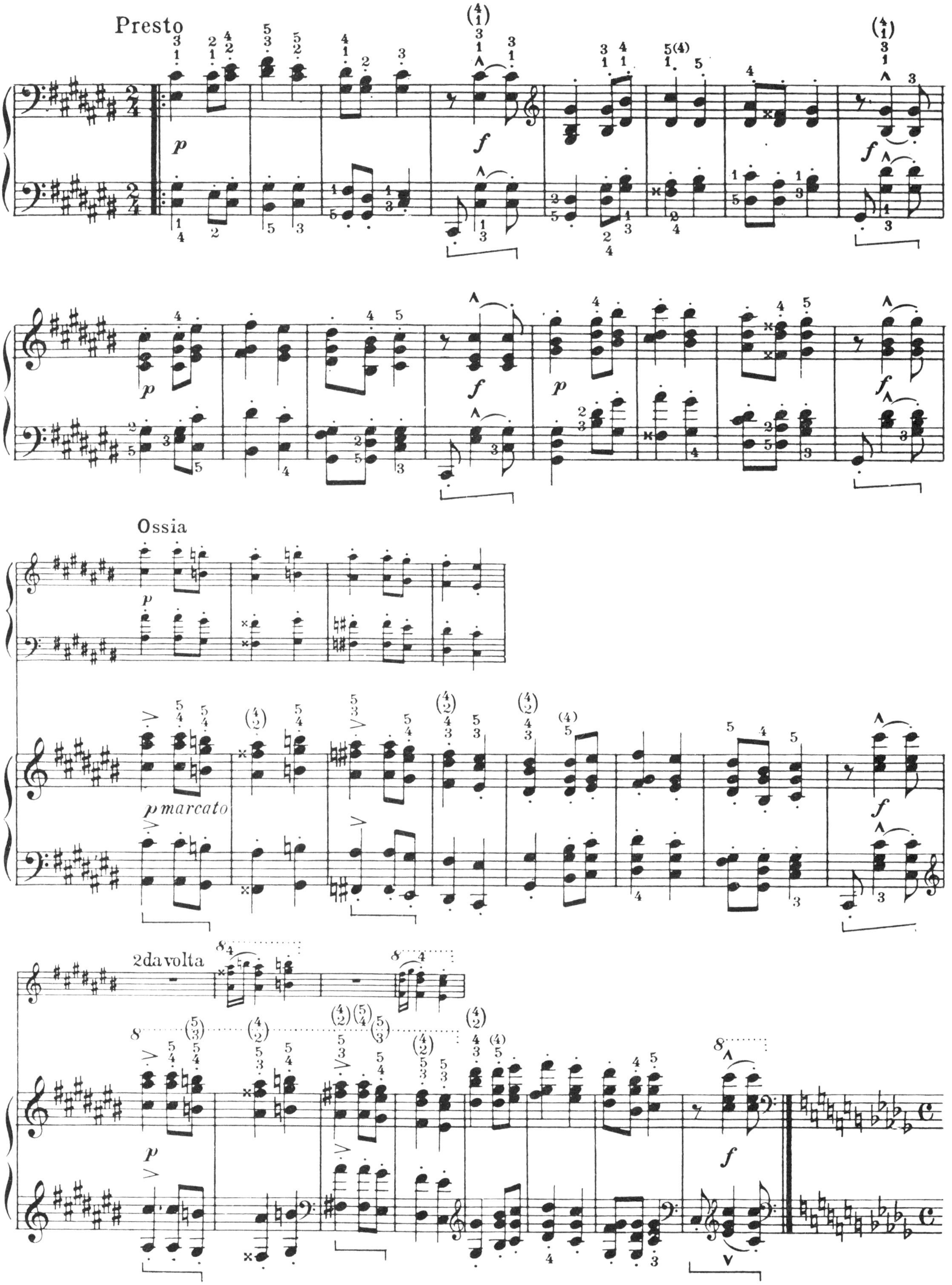
Presto
Ossia
p marcato
2da volta

Andante
mf espressivo
p
riten. a piacere
rit.
più f
sempre espress.
delicato
tr
p
mf
p

N.B. – *Two treatments of this Cadenza are given* { *Original – right hand only – fingering above* { *Optional – both hands – left hand notes with stems down – fingering below for both hands*

ten.
sempre dolce, leggieramente e stacc.
ten.
ten.
più cresc.
poco calando
ten.
ten.
riten.

legg.
Ossia Facilité
smorz.
a tempo
p
sempre staccato
etc.
sempre piano

dolciss.
cresc.
più cresc.
rinforz. molto
f
stacc.
f sempre
mf
stacc.

leggiero
rinforz.
rinforz.
più rinforz. e string.
Presto
sempre ff
stacc.

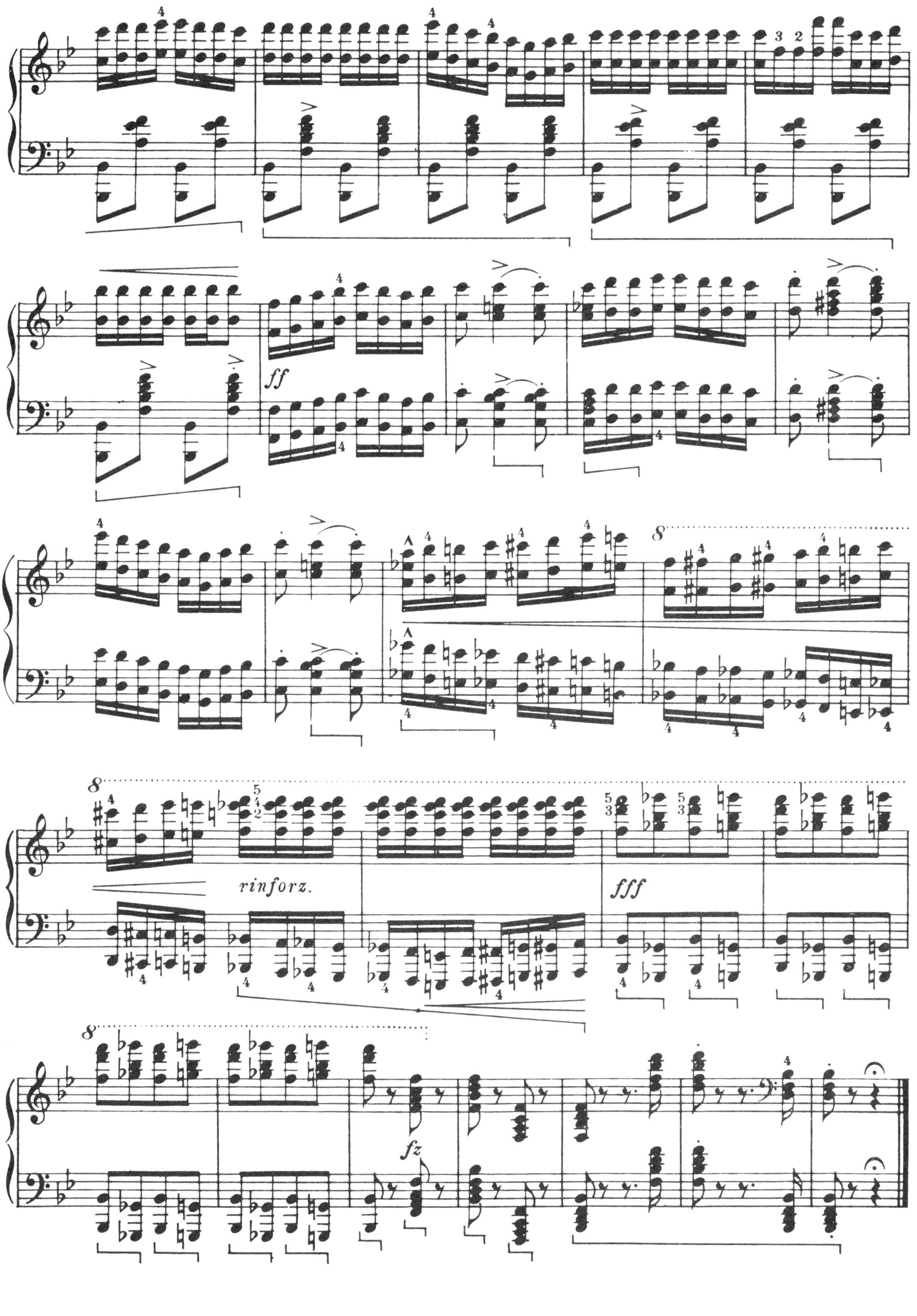
ff
rinforz.
fff
fz

LA REGATTA VENETIANA
(Nocturne)

Franz Liszt
(1811-1886)

Allegro moderato (♪ = 192)

p dolce
delicatamente
rall. un poco
f energico
p
ten.
rf.
ten.
p
f marcato
ten.
pp

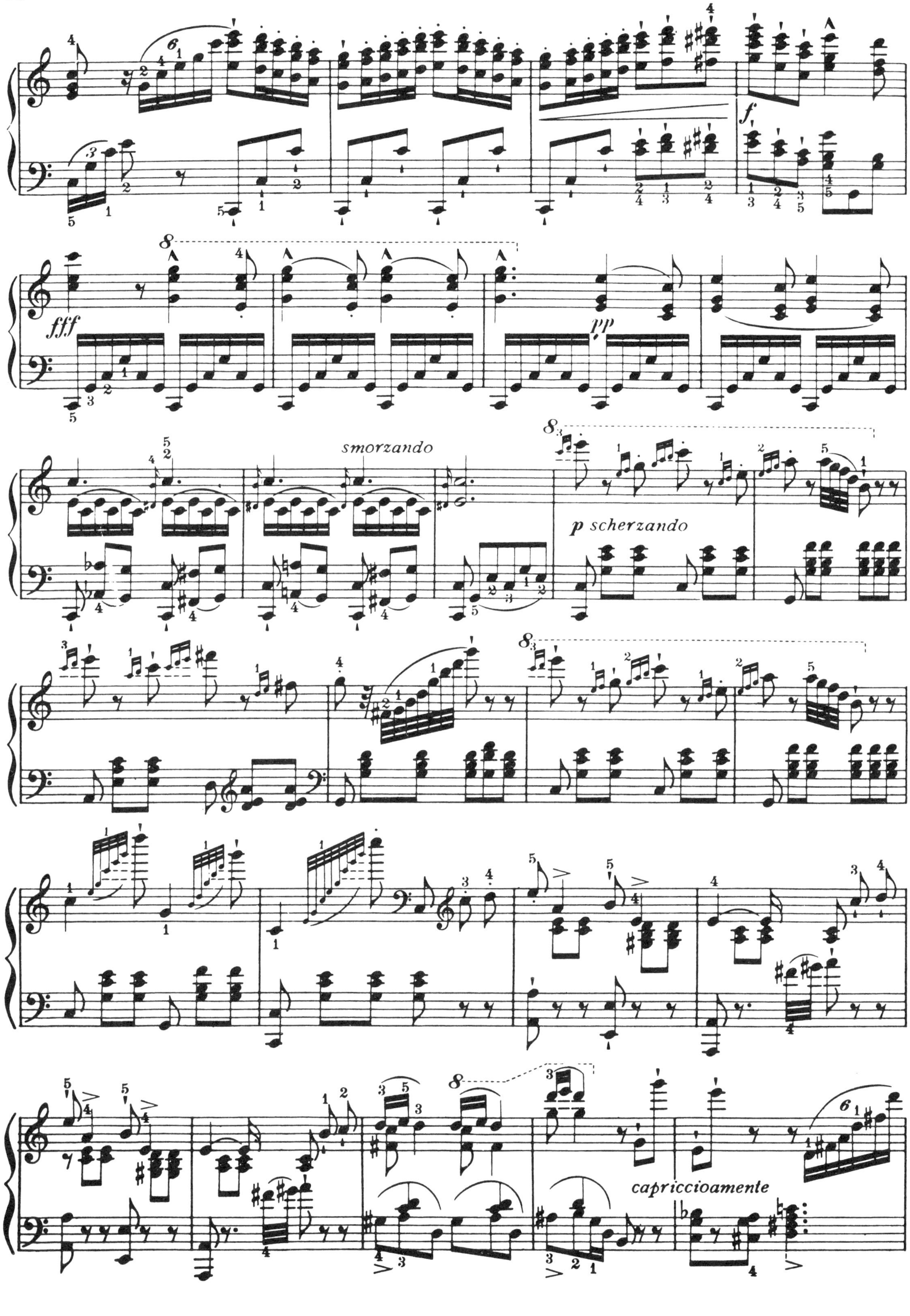

fff
pp
smorzando
p scherzando
f
capriccioamente

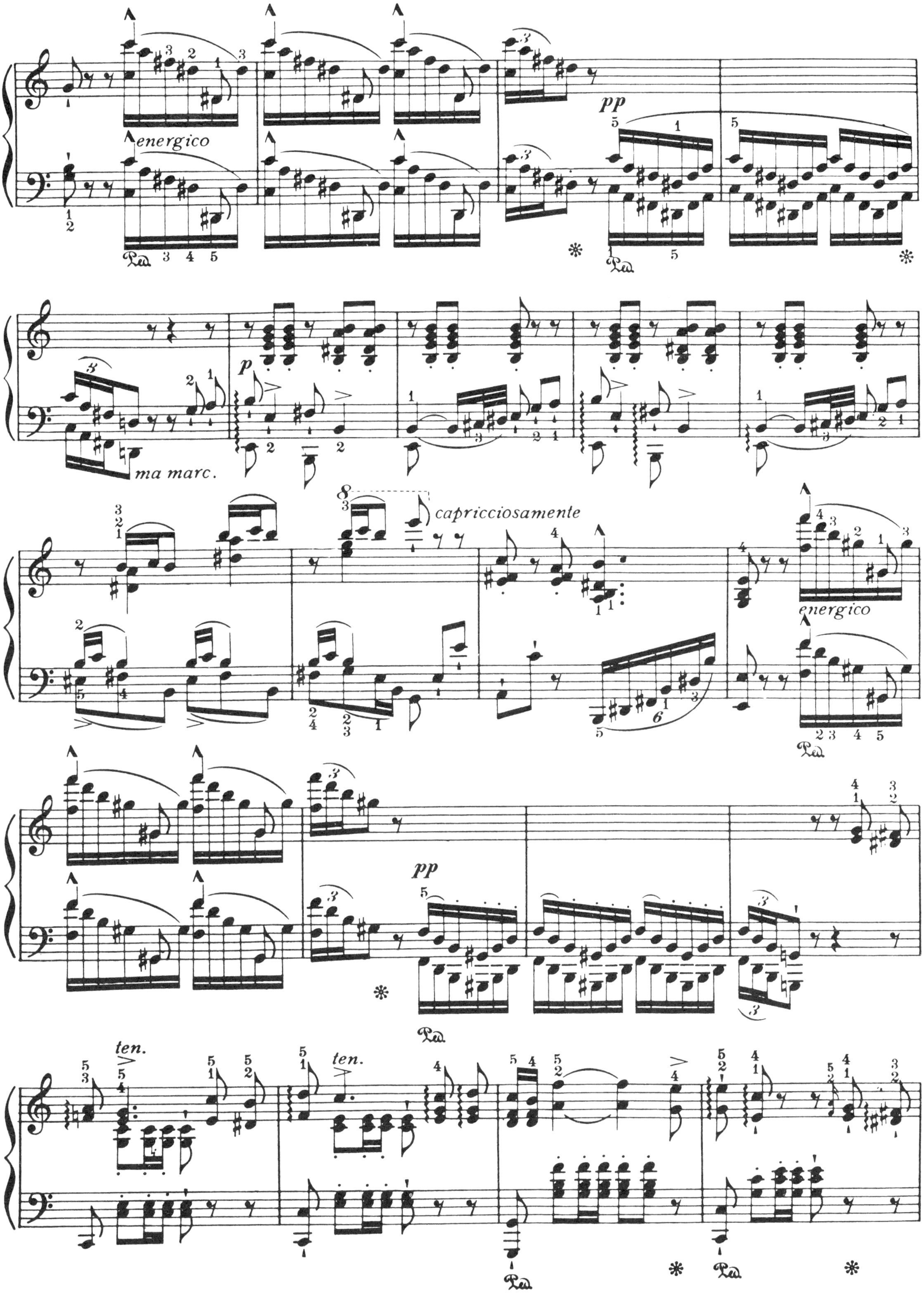
energico
pp
ma marc.
p
capricciosamente
energico
pp
ten.
ten.

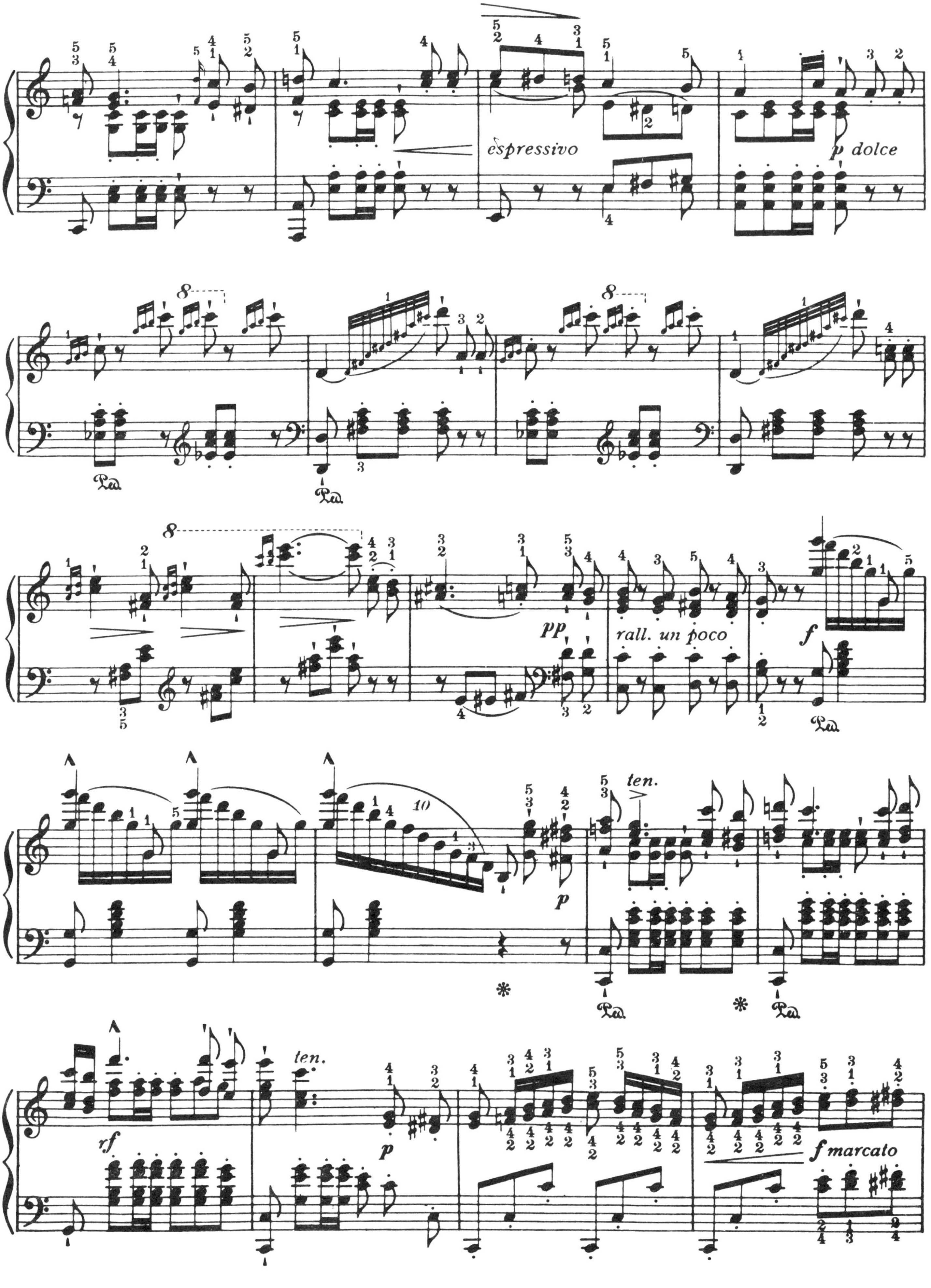
espressivo
p dolce
rall. un poco
ten.
rf
ten.
f marcato

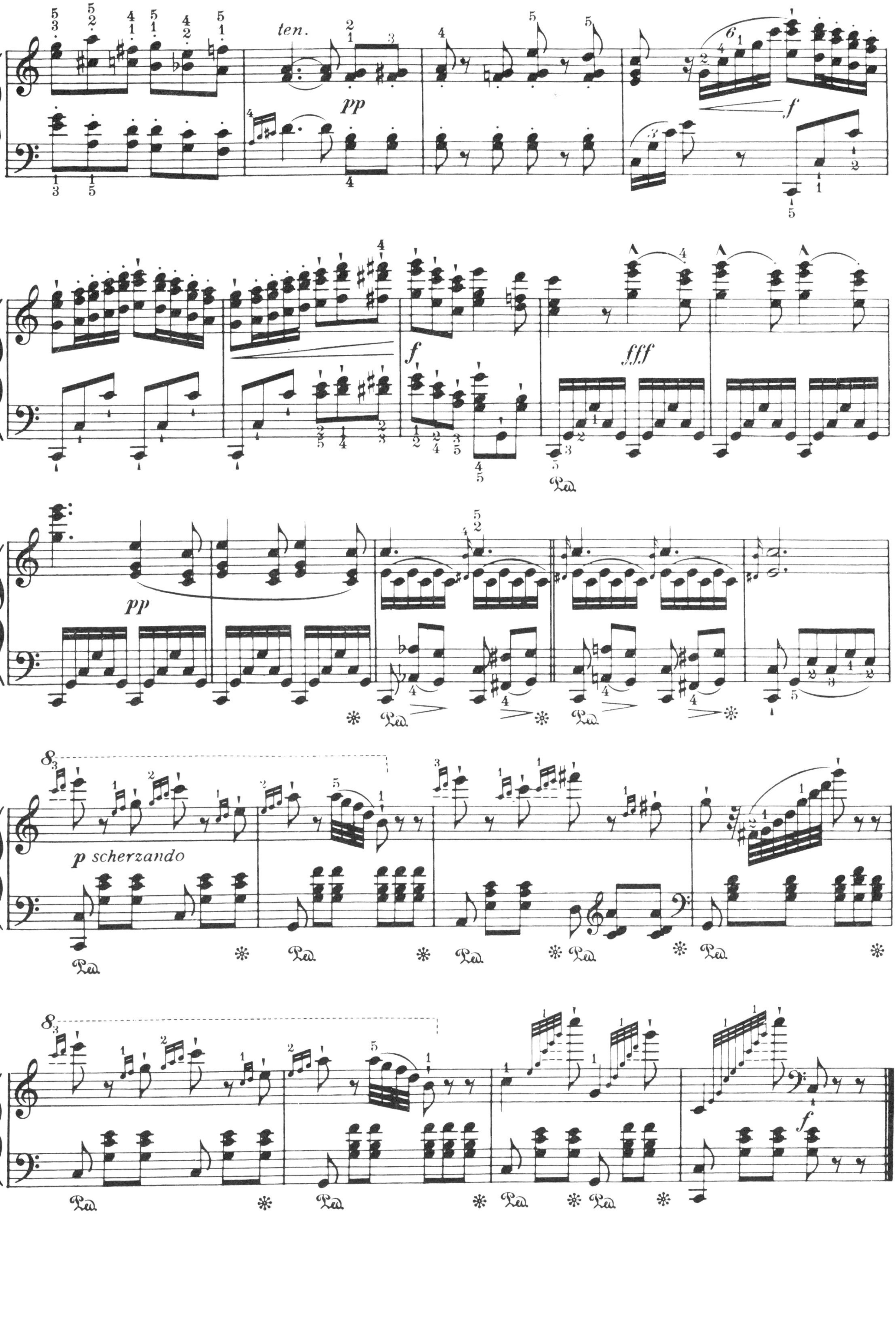
ten.
pp
f
f
fff
pp
p scherzando
f

LIEBESTRAUM NO. 1

Franz Liszt
(1811-1886)

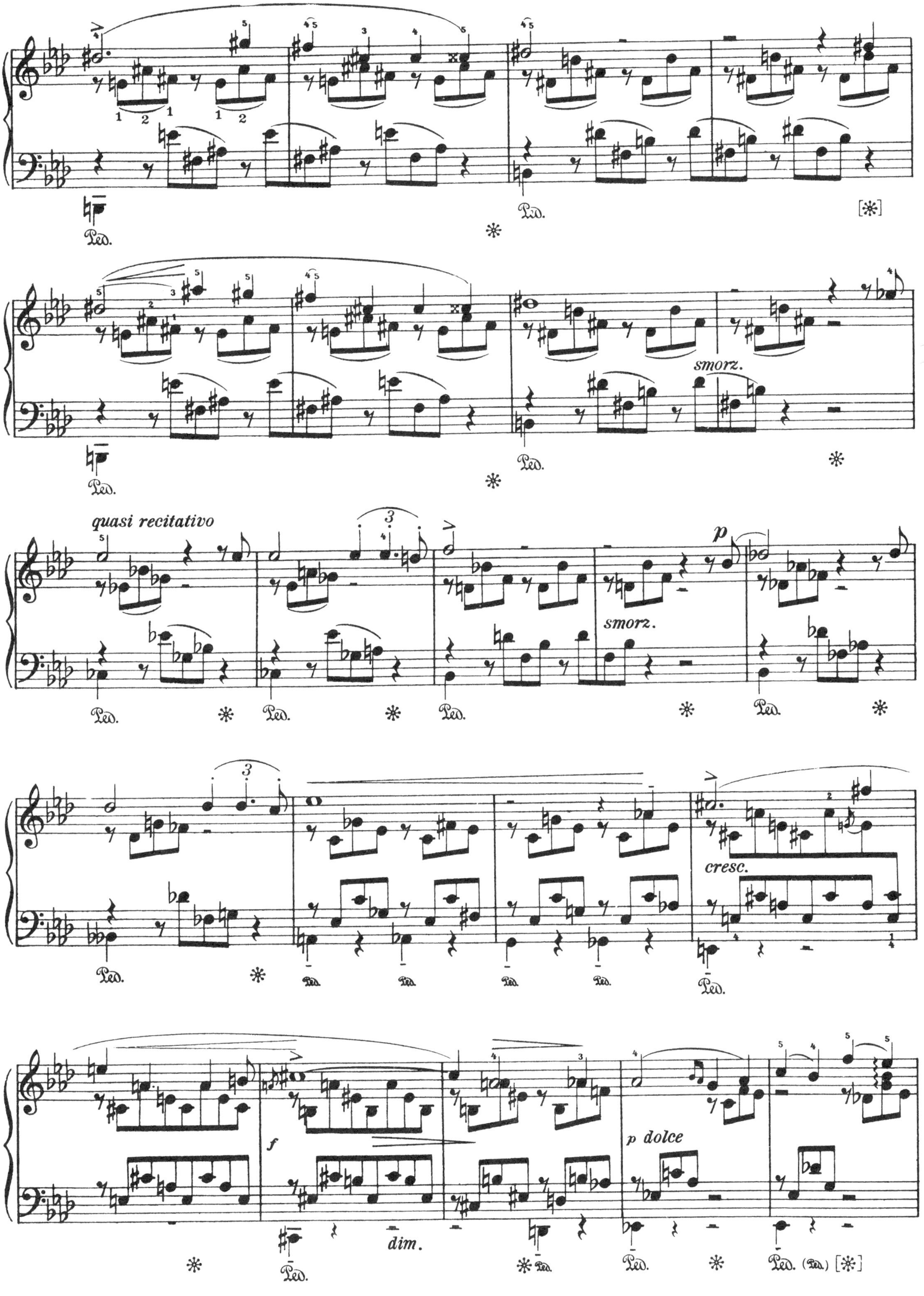
smorz.
quasi recitativo
smorz.
p
cresc.
f
dim.
p dolce

cresc. e un poco agitato
rinforz.
smorz.
pp
riten.
molto
quasi Arpa
pp
a tempo
mf il canto espressivo assai
pp
p sempre una corda
pp

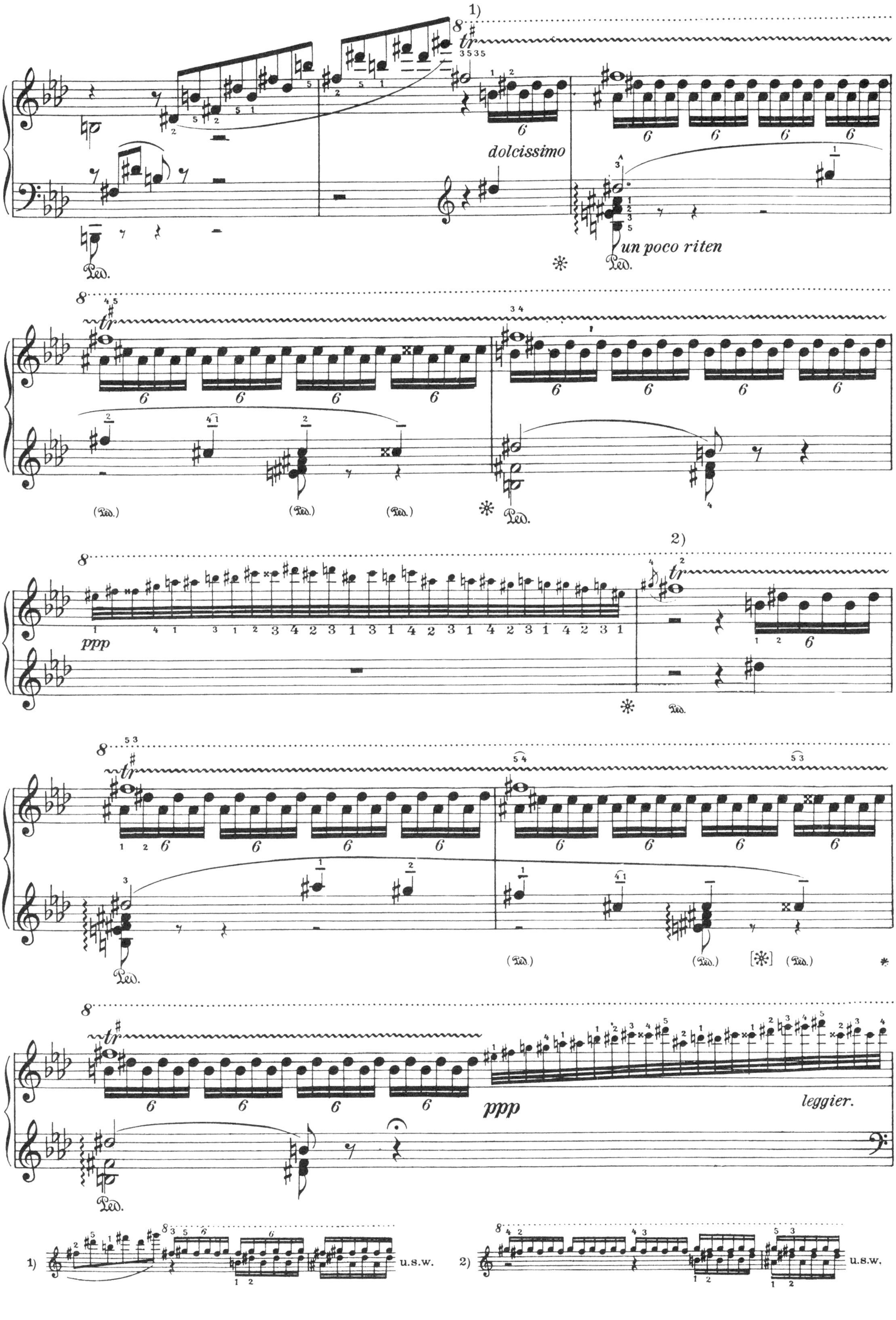
1)
dolcissimo
un poco riten
2)
ppp
ppp
leggier.
1)
u.s.w.
2)
u.s.w.

p
pp
quasi recitativo
cresc.
p dolce
espressivo
poco ritard.
smorz.
dolce
cresc.
mf
rinfz.
marcato

smorz.
placido
appassionato
rit.
dolcissimo
a tempo
languendo
accentato assai
poco rit.

LIEBESTRAUM NO. 2

Franz Liszt
(1811-1886)

Quasi lento, abbandonandosi

mf
p
mf
p
p
pp
pp
p
riten.
smorz.
sempre marcato il canto
armonioso
dolcissimo

un poco animato
f grandioso
string.
cresc.
rinforz. appassionato assai
ff
dim.
mf
rit.
rinforz.
con passione
f

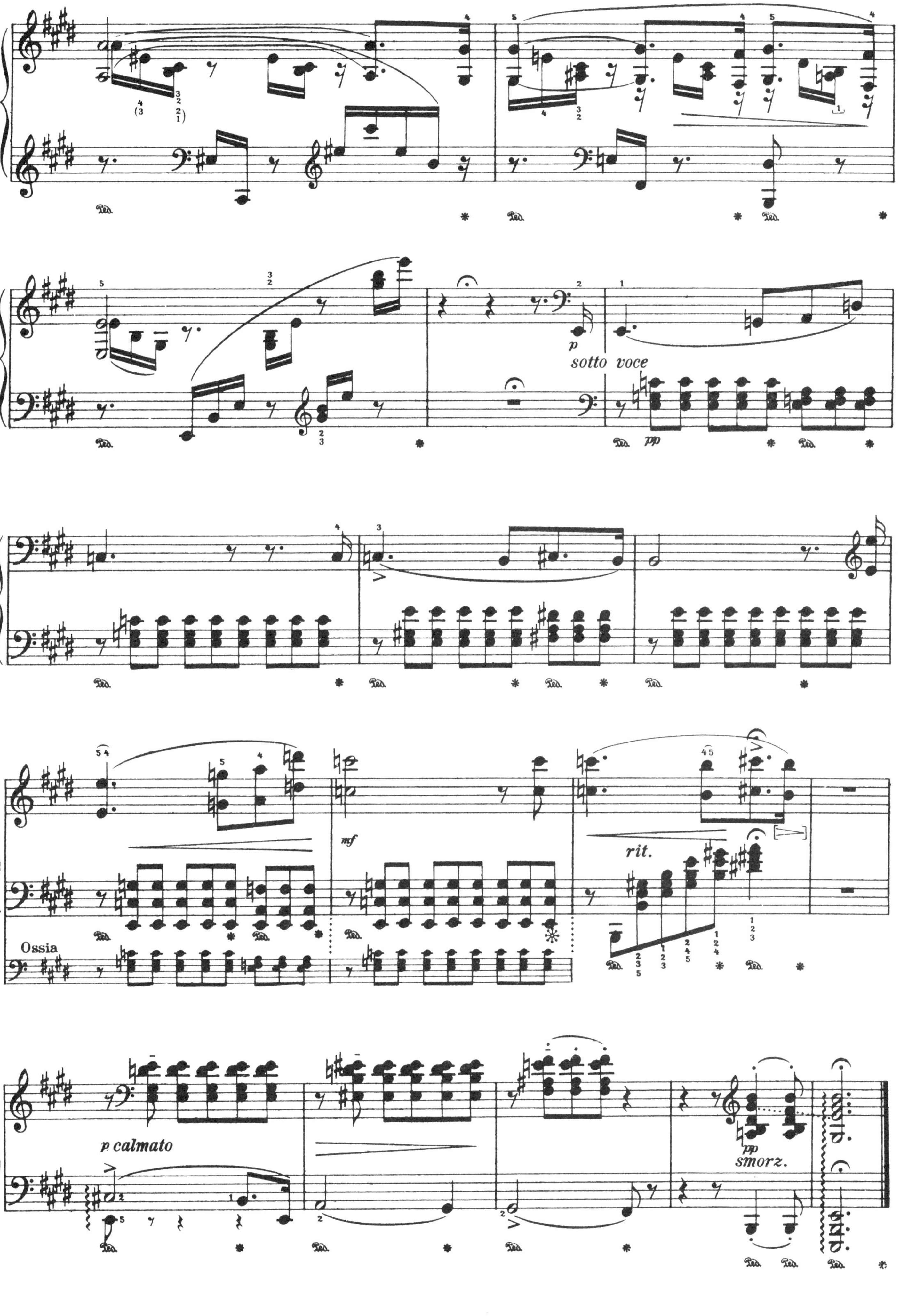
p
sotto voce
pp
mf
rit.
Ossia
p calmato
pp
smorz.

LIEBESTRAUM NO. 3

Franz Liszt
(1811-1886)

Poco allegro, con affetto

dolce cantando

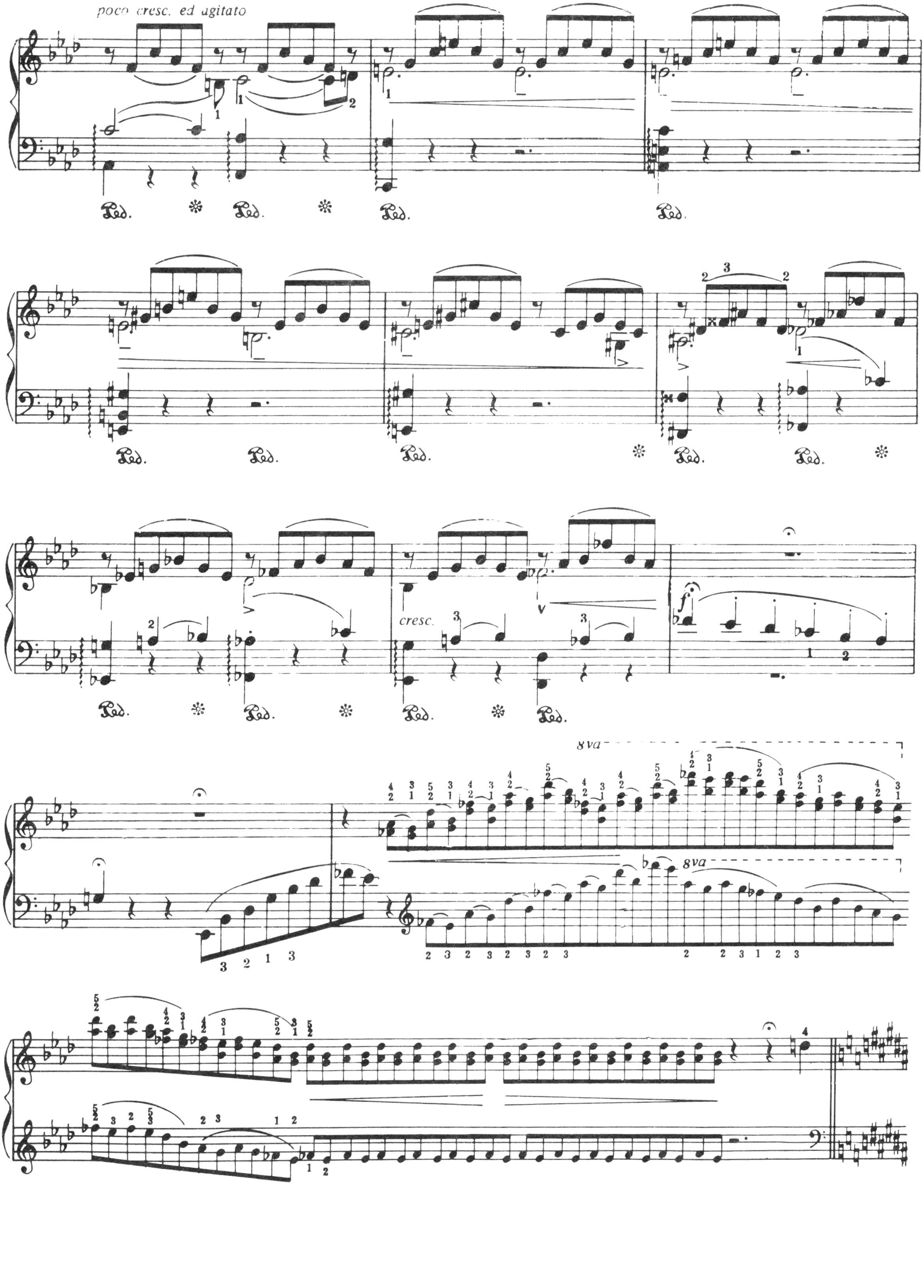
poco cresc. ed agitato
Ped.
cresc.
8va
f

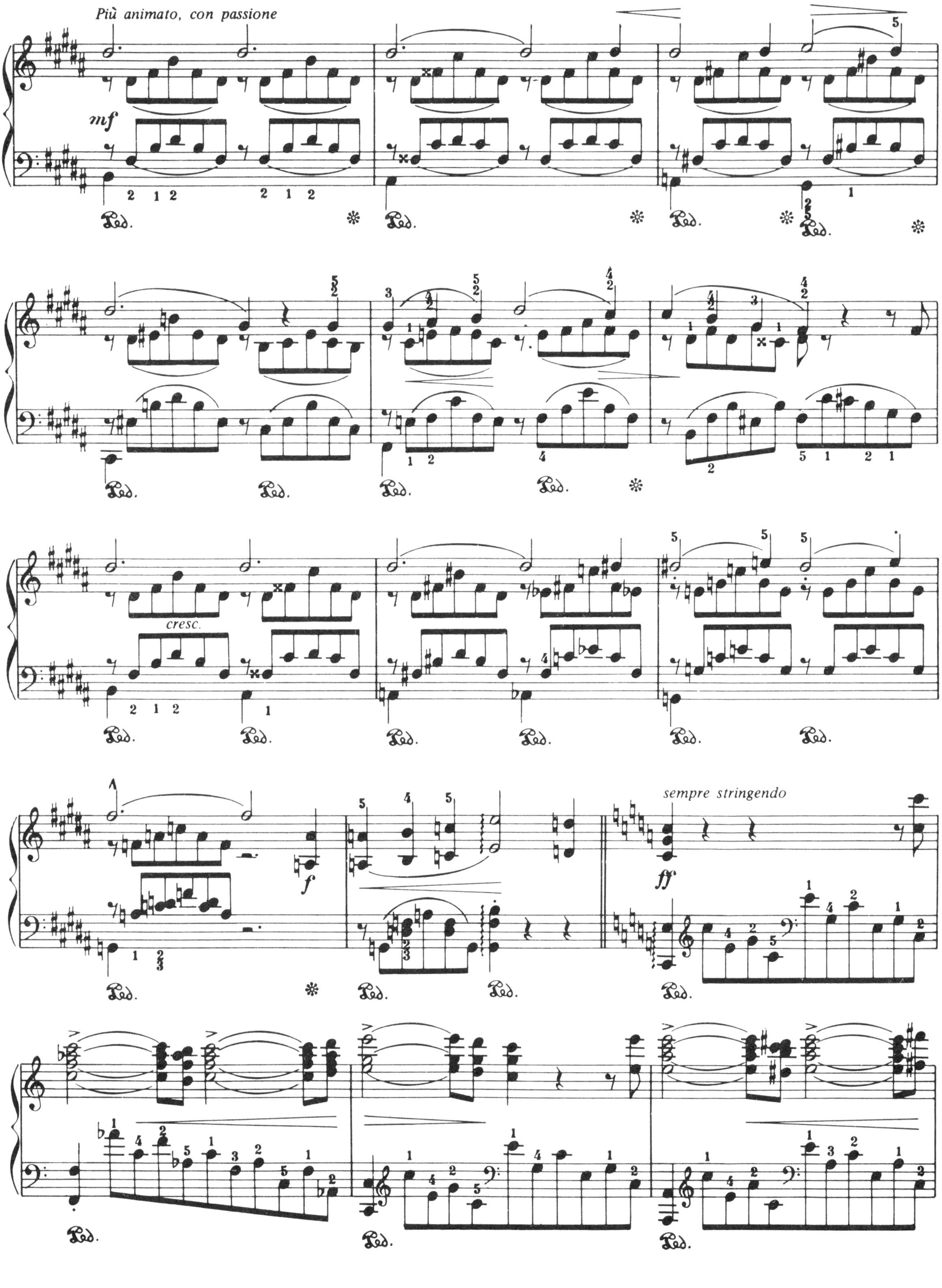
Più animato, con passione
cresc.
sempre stringendo

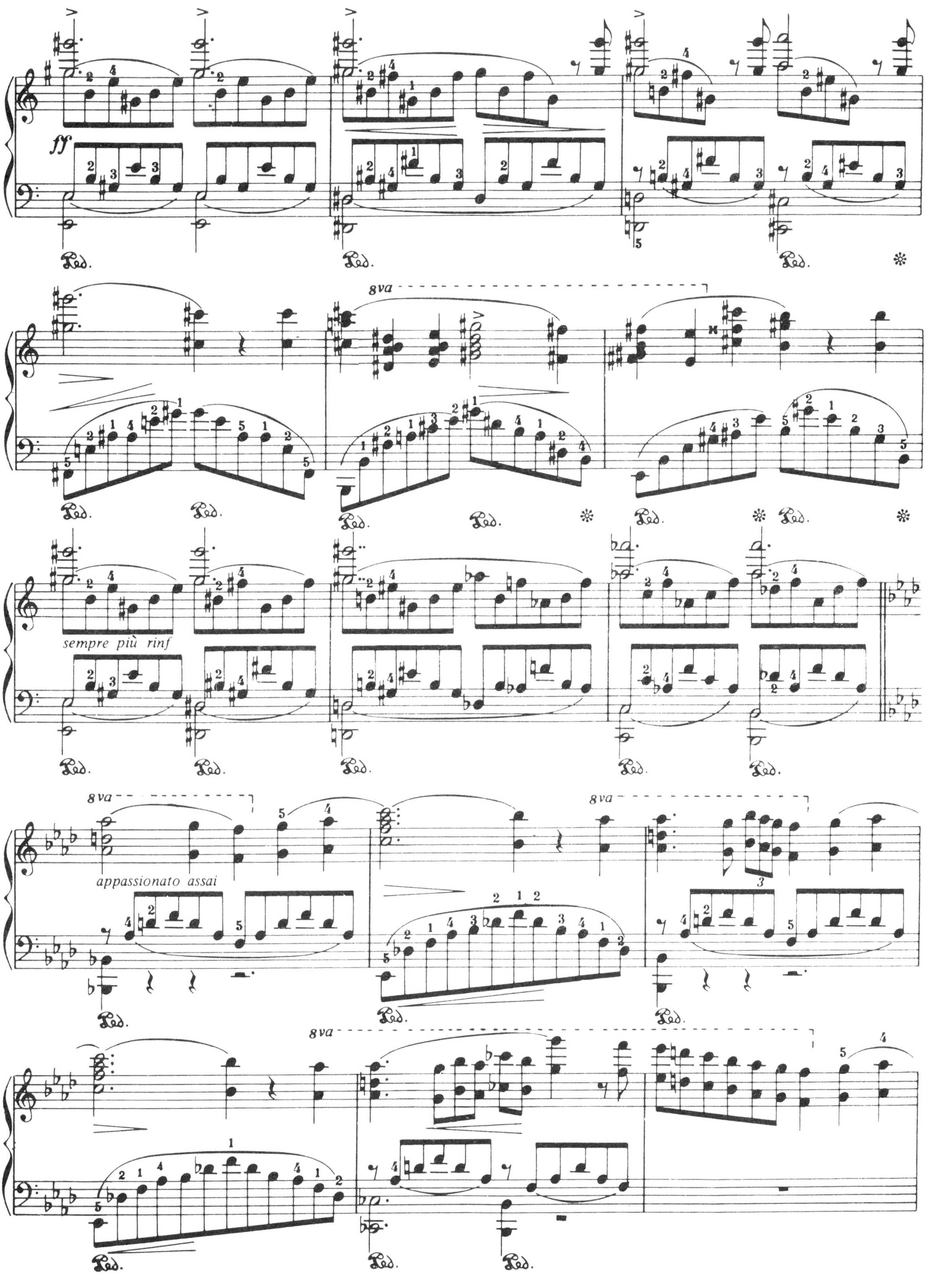
ff
Ped.
8va
sempre più rinf
appassionato assai

8va
affrettando
Ped.
Ped.
8va
8va
dim.
Ped.
Ped.
8va
leggiero
ritard
Tempo primo
p
dolce
armonioso
Ped.
Ped.
Ped.
Ped.
Ped.

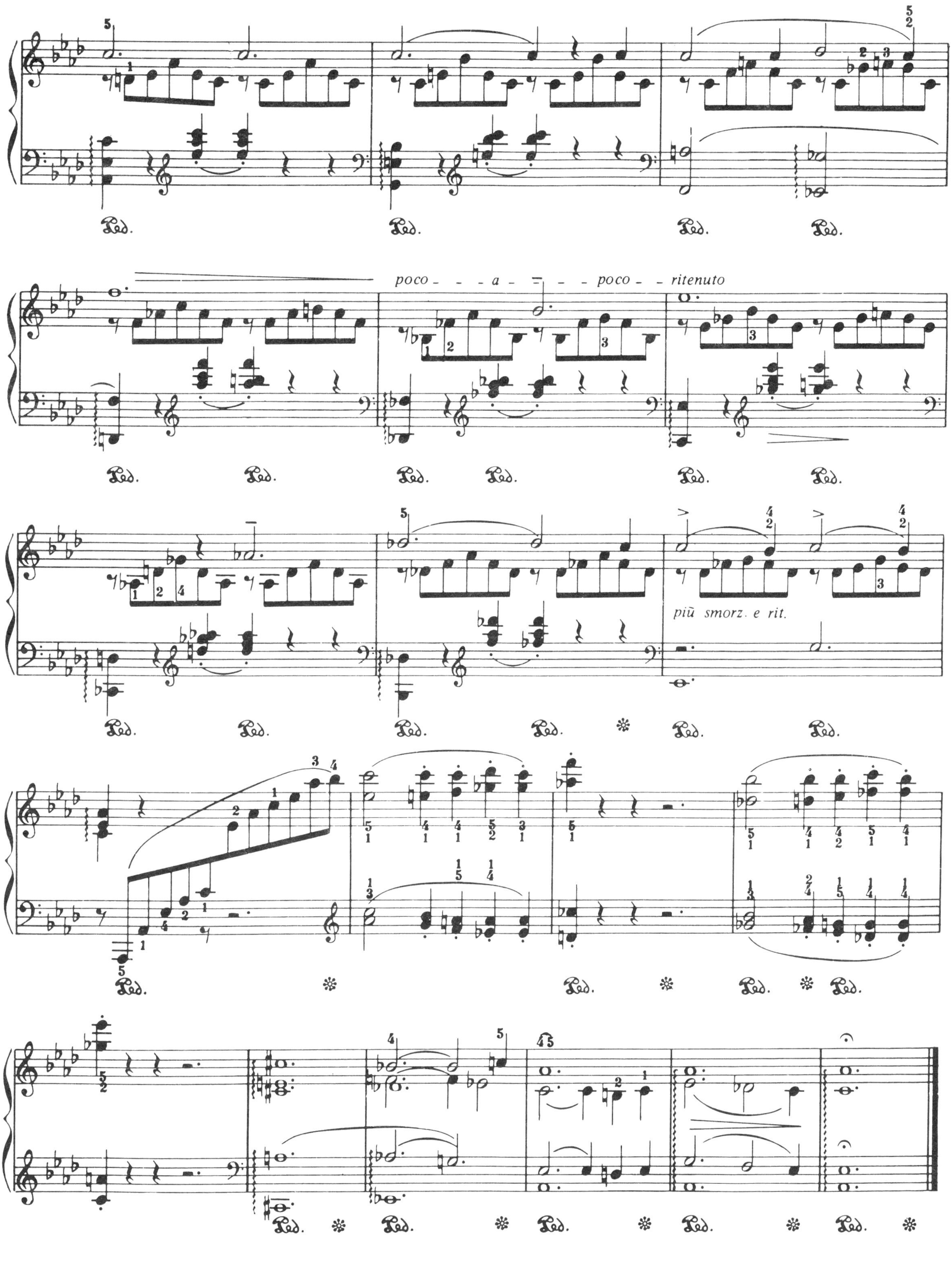
poco - - - a - - - poco - - ritenuto
più smorz. e rit.

MEPHISTO WALTZ
(Theme)

Franz Liszt
(1811-1886)

(Tempo mosso di Valse, ma con espressione soave)

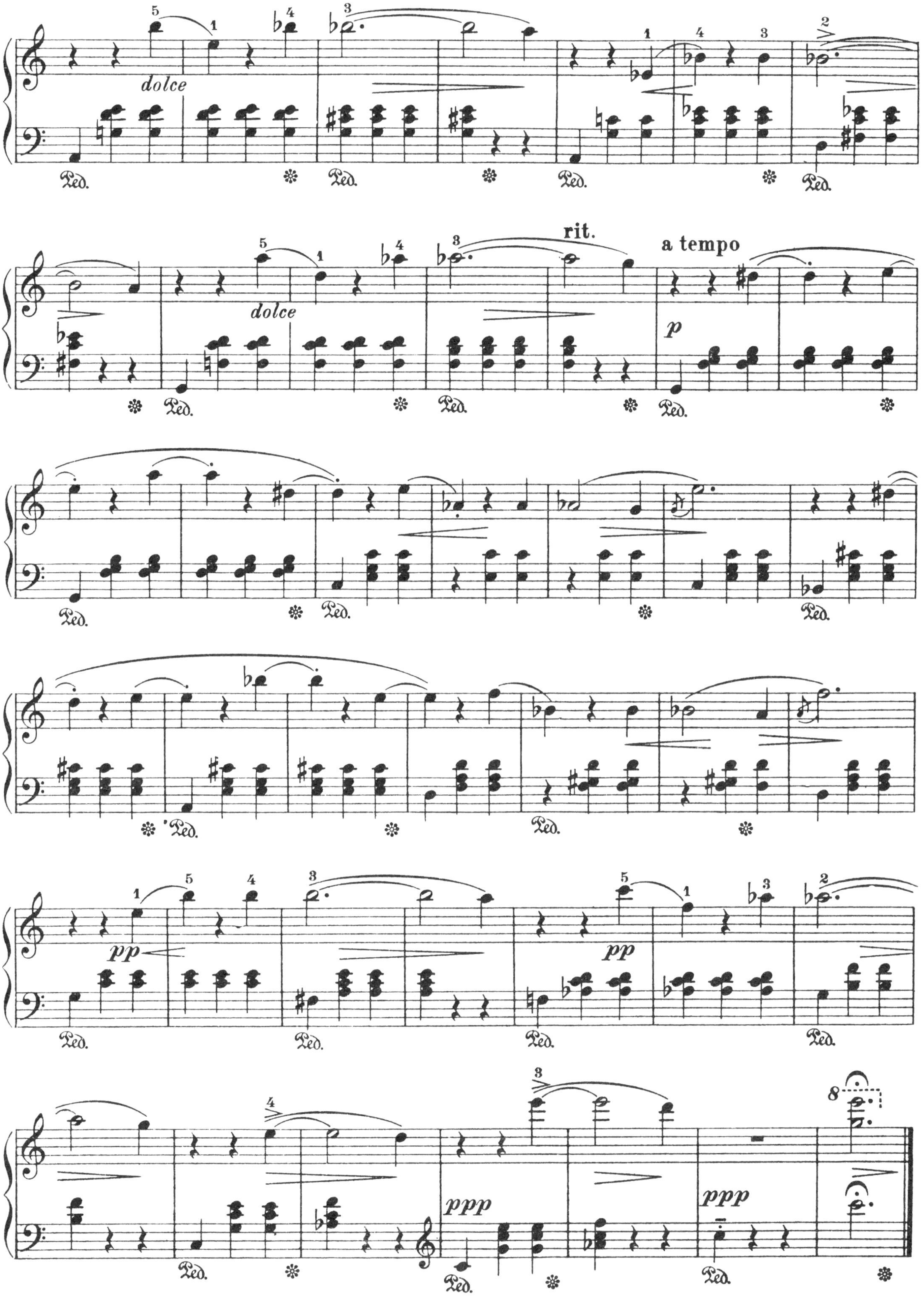
dolce
Ped.
rit.
a tempo
p
pp
ppp
8

NOCTURNE IN B
(En Reve)

Franz Liszt
(1811-1886)

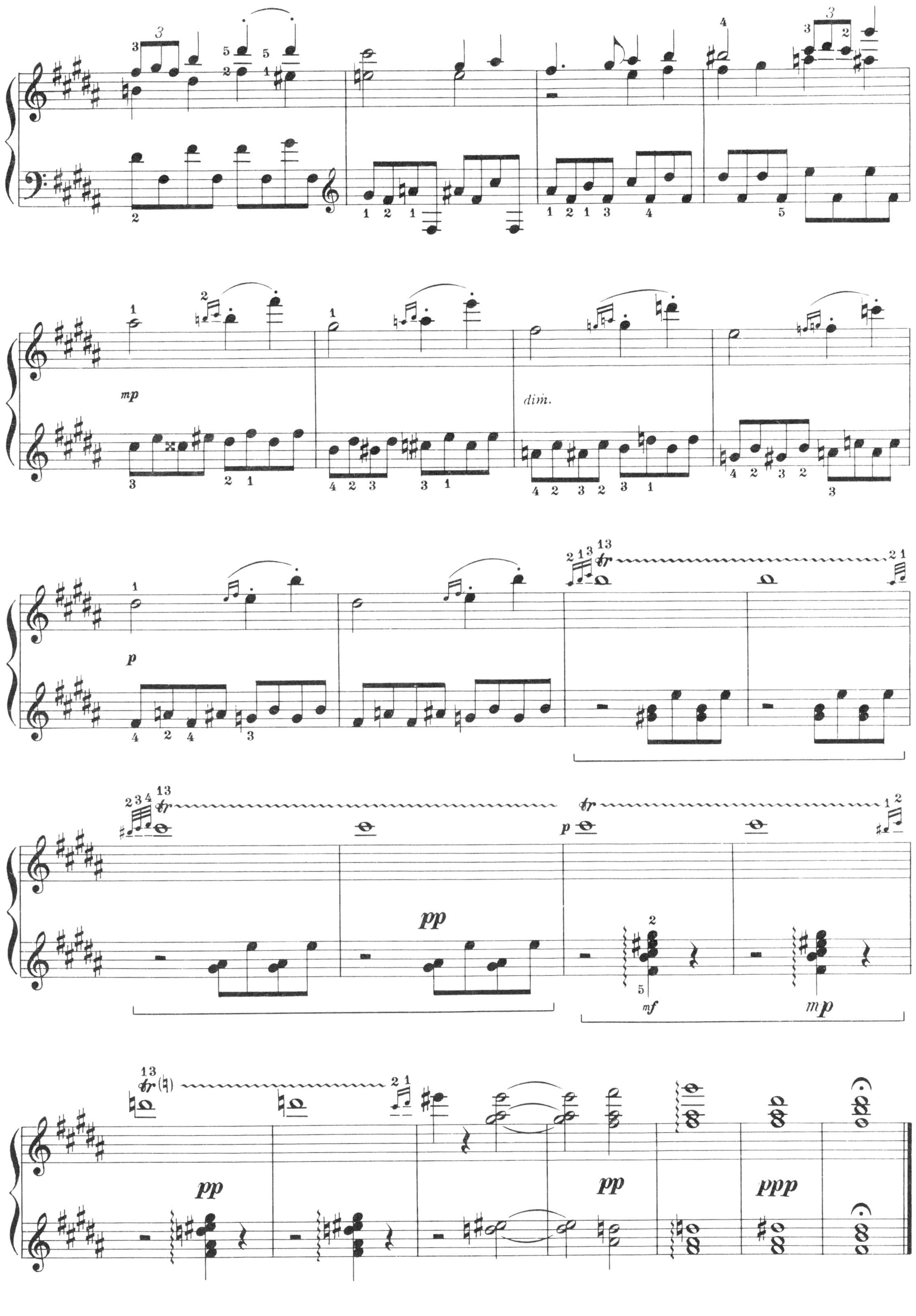
mp
dim.
p
pp
p
mf
mp
pp
pp
ppp

NUAGES GRIS

Franz Liszt
(1811-1886)

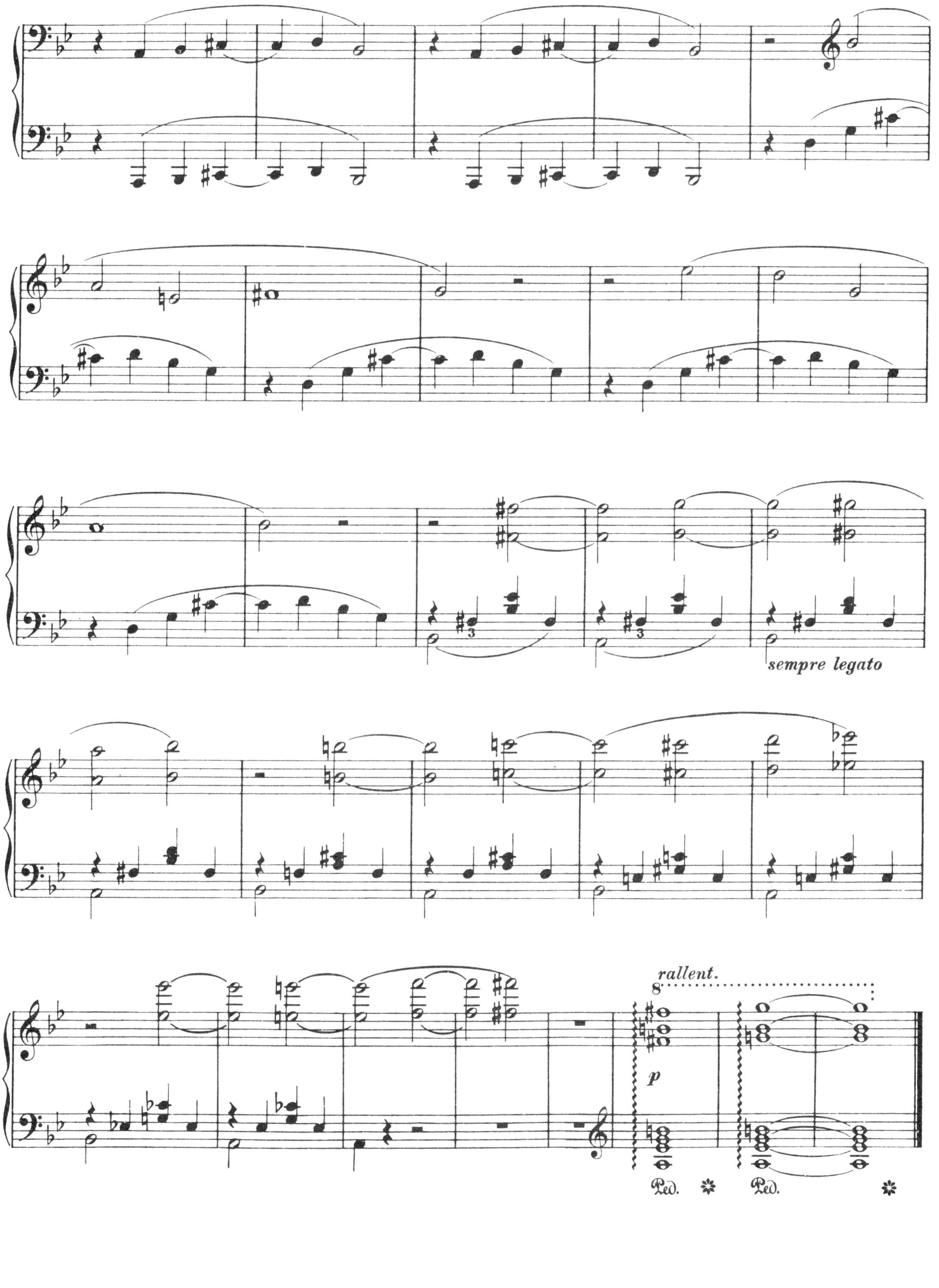
sempre legato
rallent.
p
Ped.
Ped.

VALSE MELANCOLIQUE

Franz Liszt
(1811-1886)

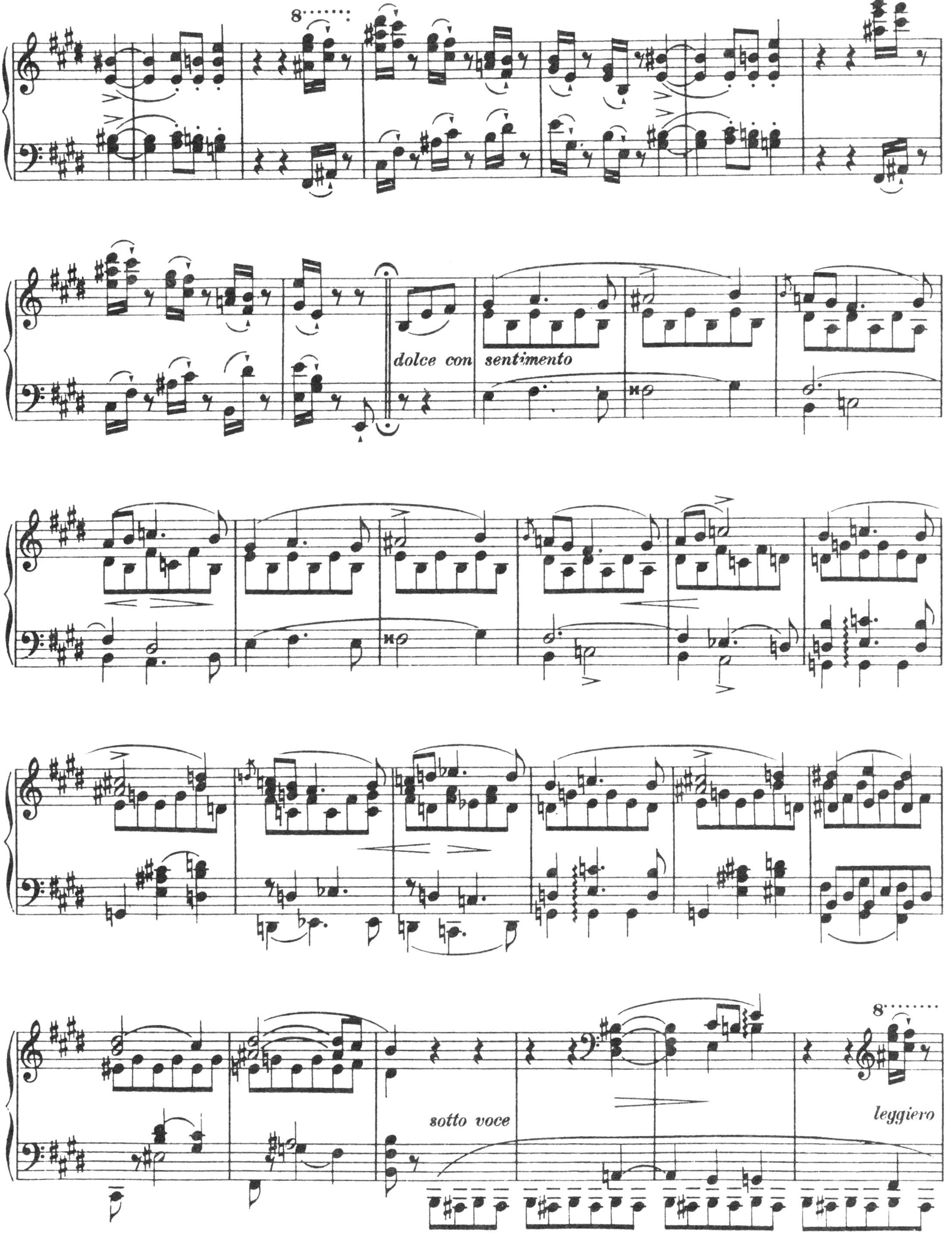
dolce con sentimento
sotto voce
leggiero

scherzando
accelerando
sempre rubato
con molto sentimento
cresc.

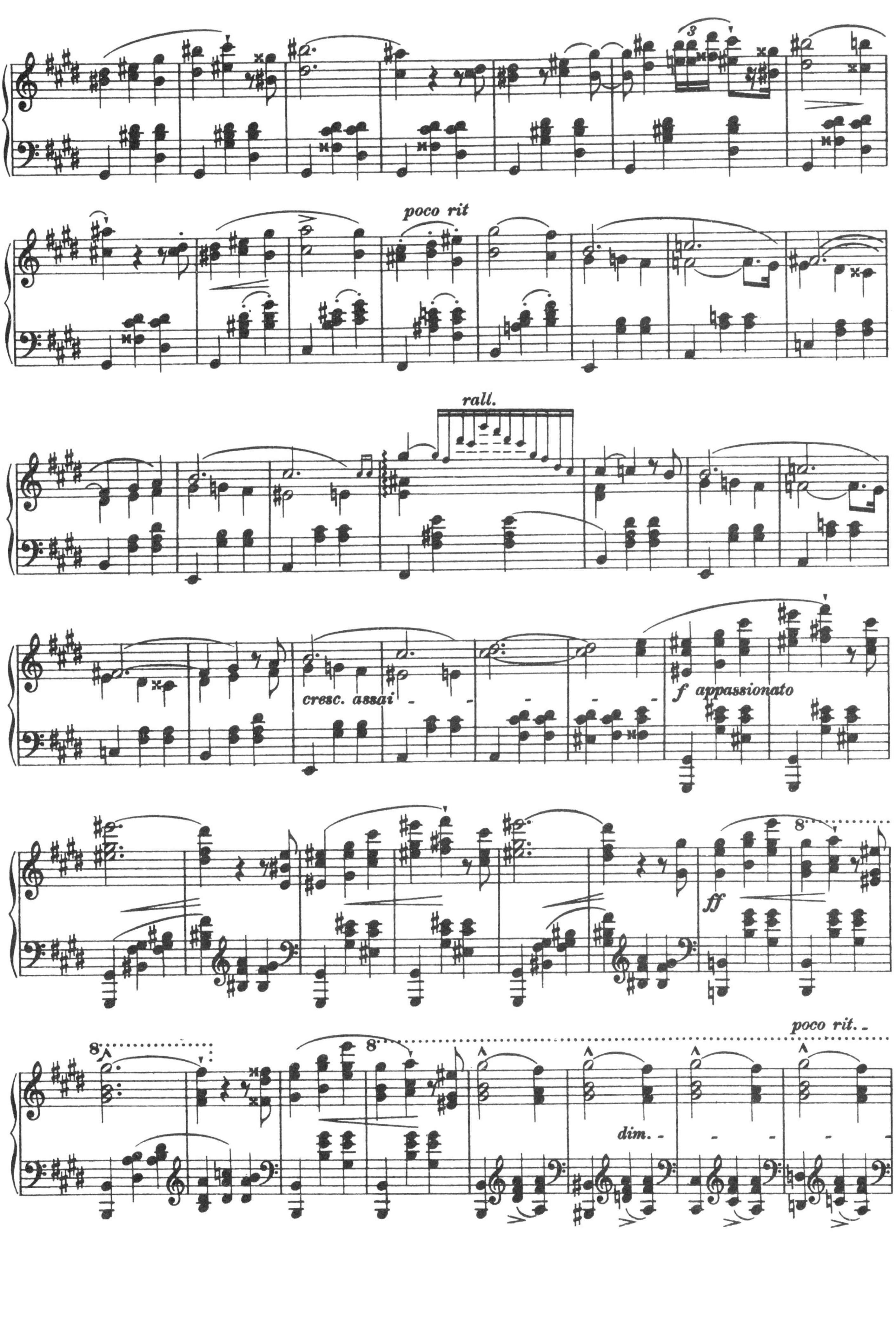
poco rit
rall.
cresc. assai
f appassionato
ff
poco rit.
dim.

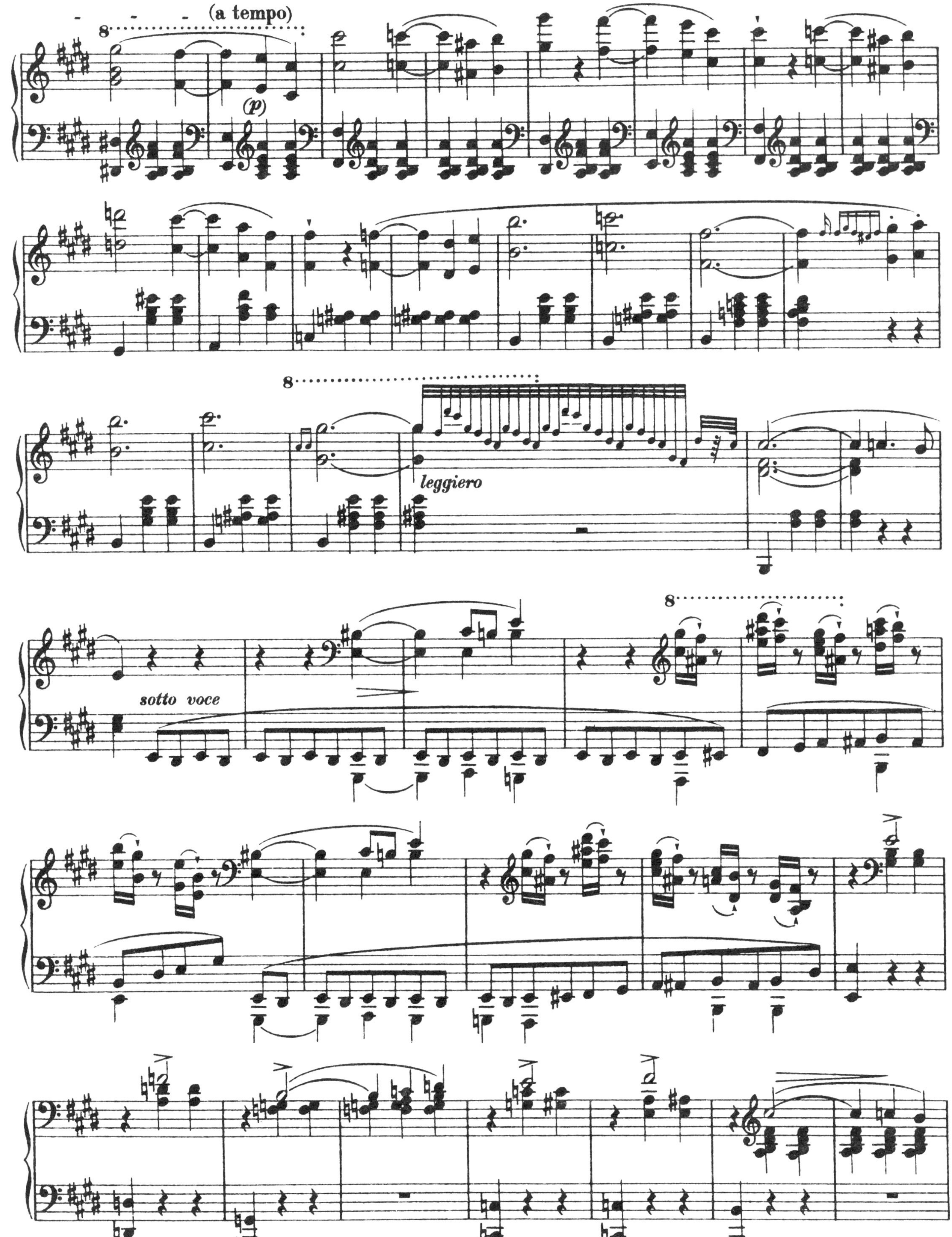
(a tempo)
(p)
leggiero
sotto voce

agitato
stringendo
cresc.
assai
poco rit.
calmato
dolce
ritenuto
5
dolce armonioso
rit.
pp

VALSE OUBLIEE NO. 1

Franz Liszt
(1811-1886)

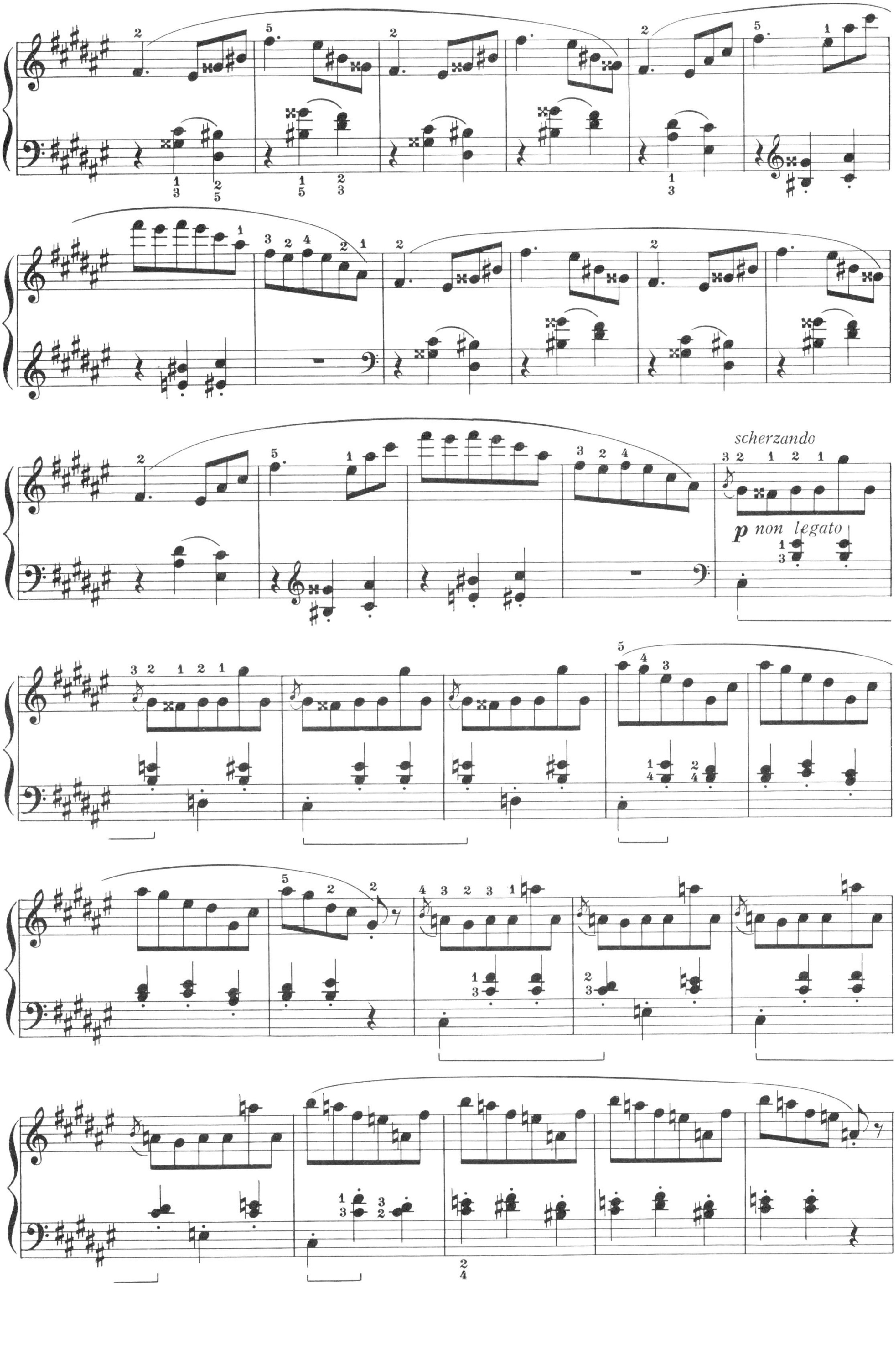
scherzando
p non legato

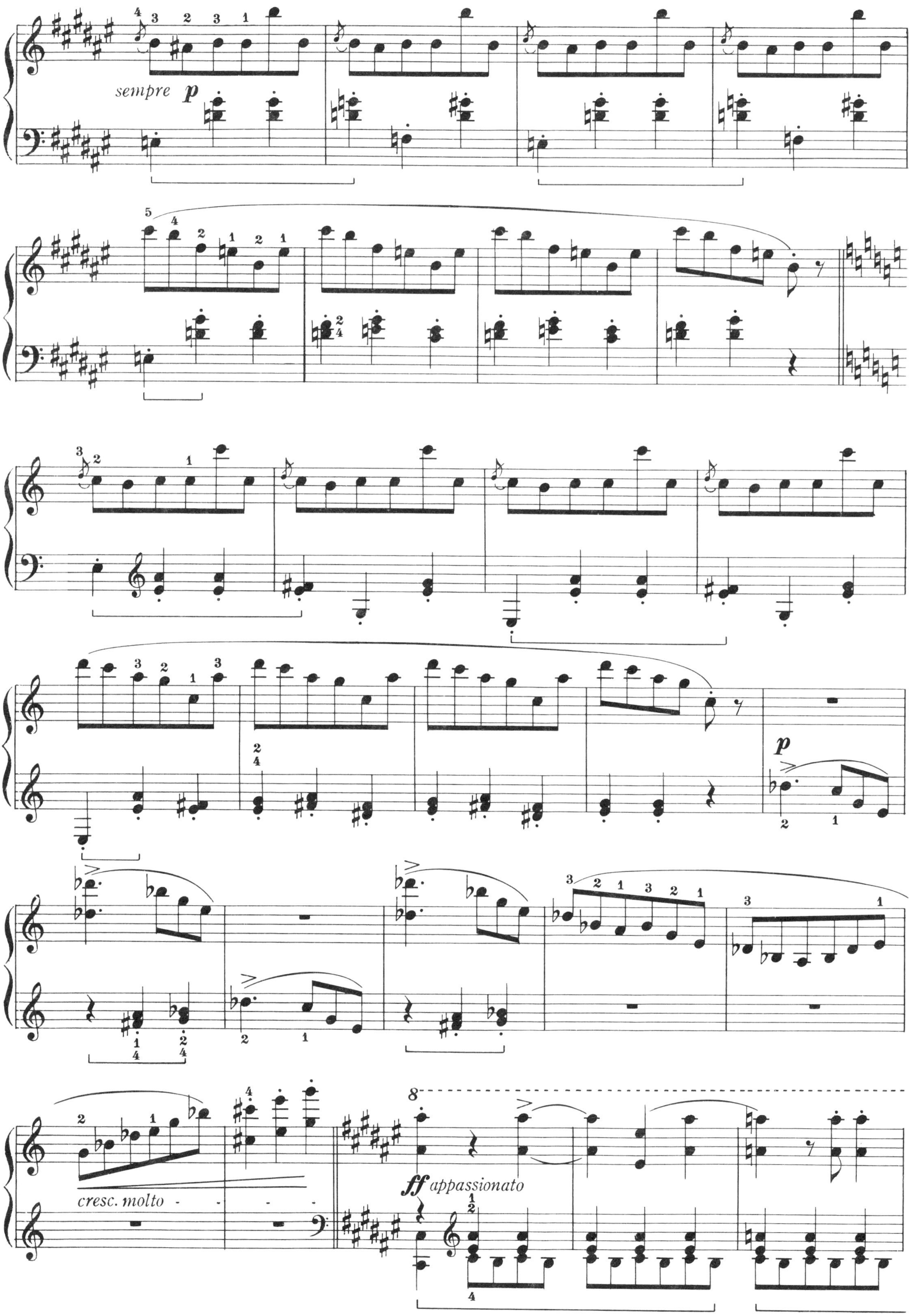
sempre p
p
cresc. molto
ff appassionato

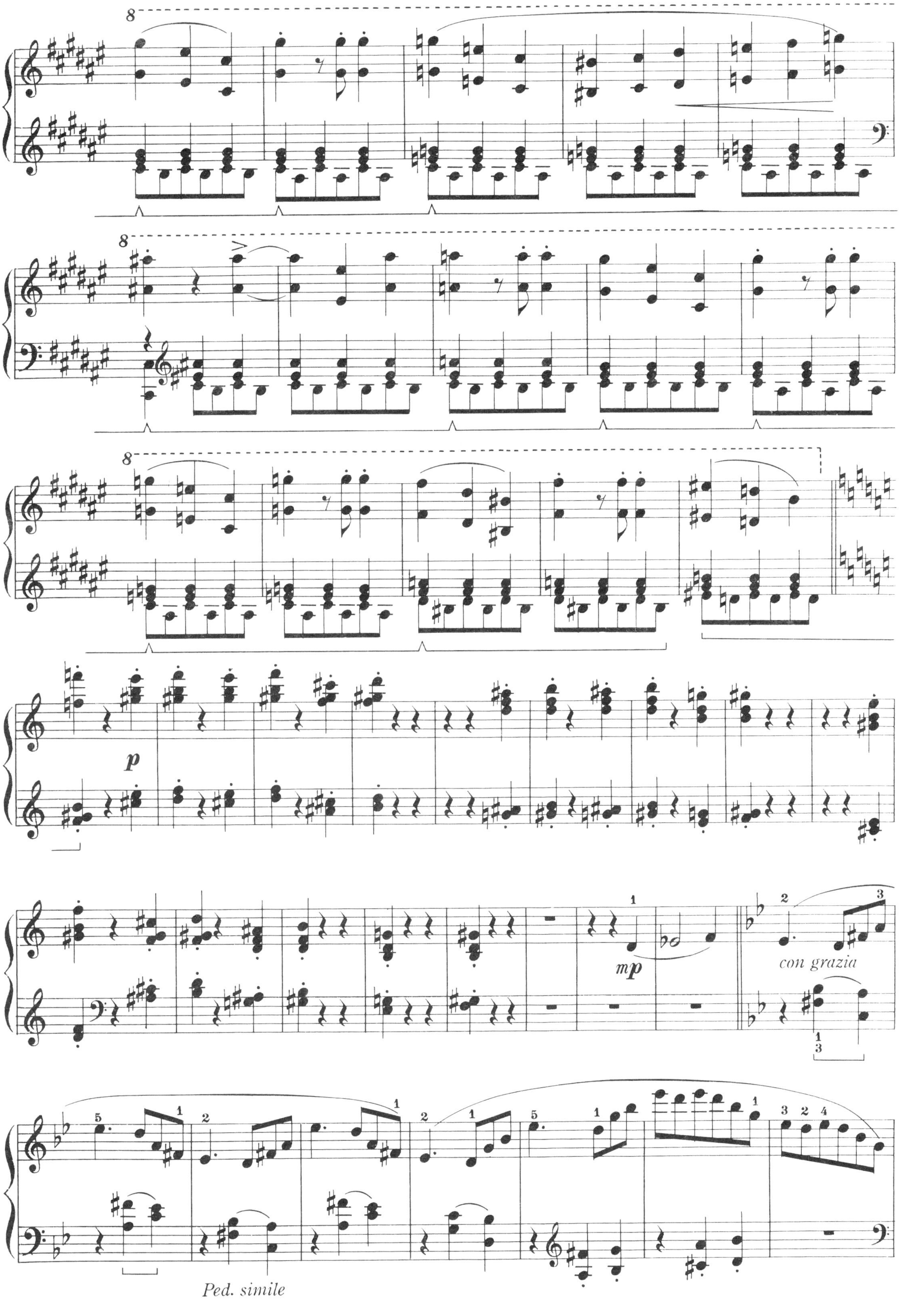
8
8
8
p
mp
con grazia
Ped. simile

senza Ped.   *p*

p amoroso

⁵*legato*
sempre con Ped.

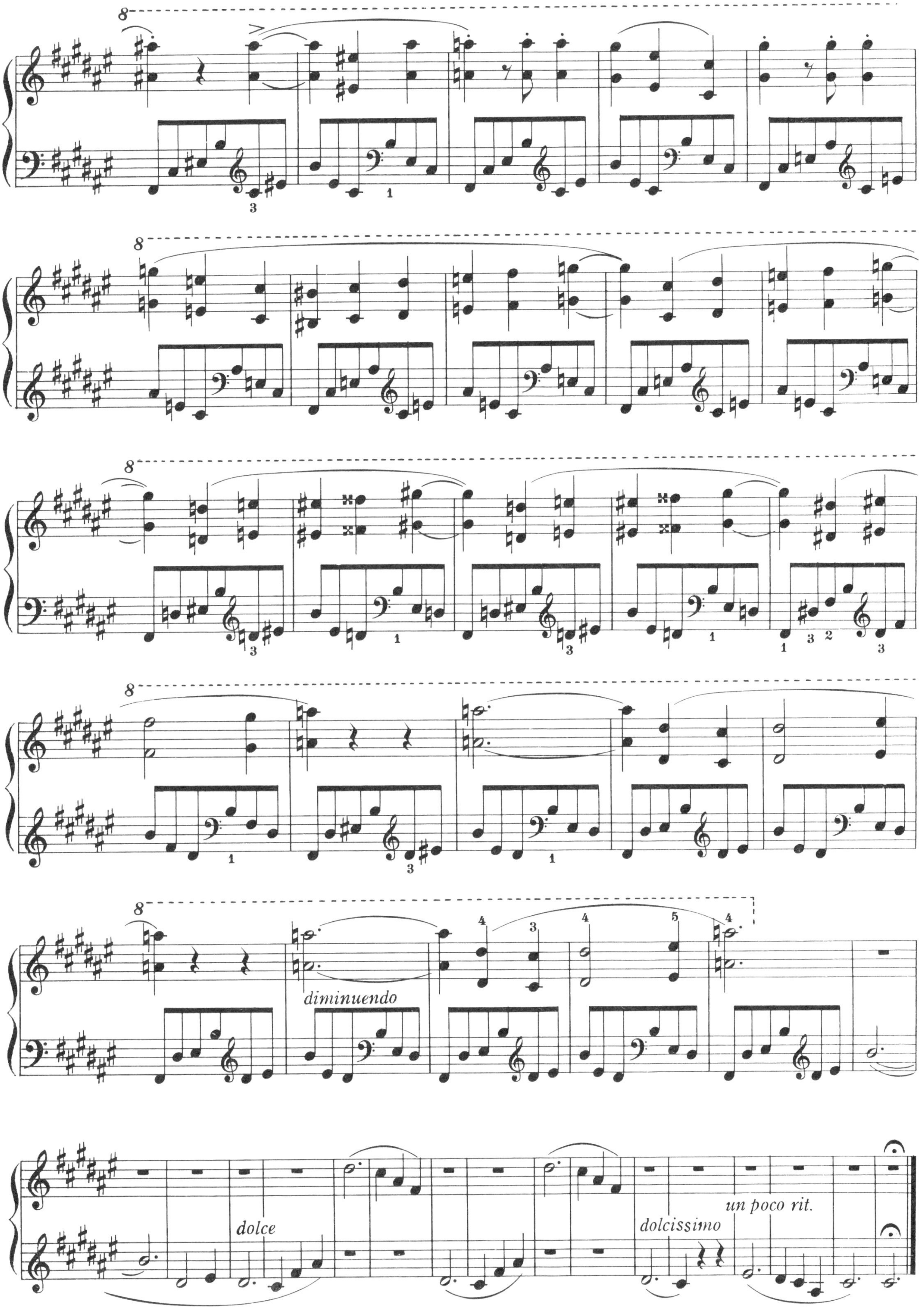
diminuendo
dolce
dolcissimo
un poco rit.

WALDESRAUSCHEN
(Konzert-Etude)

Franz Liszt
(1811-1886)

poco cresc.
poco rall. smorz. ppp
a tempo
mf
sempre legato
tre corde

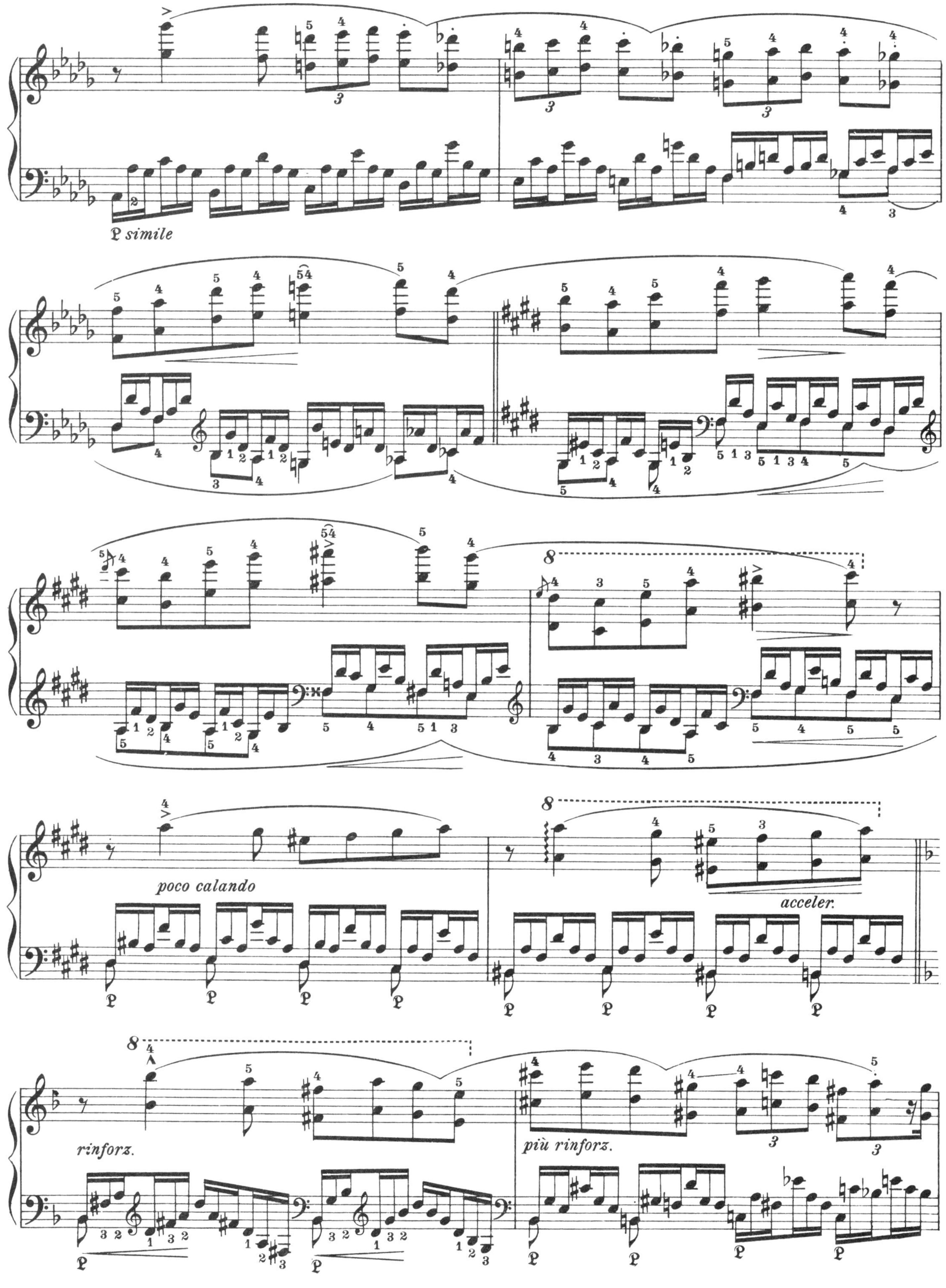
p simile
poco calando
acceler.
rinforz.
più rinforz.

leggierissimo
pp
una corda
cantando
sempre pp
cantando
pp
delicamente
poco rall.
a tempo
leggierissimo
pp
simile

pp
sempre pp
pp
delicatamente
poco a poco più agitato
tre corde
marcato
marcato
simile

sempre cresc.
ff appassionato
comminciando non troppo forte
acceler.
martellato
martellato
ten.
ten.
ten.
strepitoso
sempre cresc.
poco rall.

Un poco più mosso

ff molto appassionato

p wie früher

più rinforz.

Piano a 6 Ottave
string. molto e sempre fortissimo ed appassionato
Ossia
string. molto e sempre fortissimo ed appassionato
sf
marc.
simile
quasi trillo
simile
dim.
espress.
riten. molto

a tempo
dolcissimo e legatissimo
wie anfangs
sempre pp
perdendosi
ppp